Checklist for Life
for Teachers

Presented To:

_____

Presented By:

_____

Date:

_____

Checklist for Life
for Teachers

Checklist for Life
for Teachers

NELSON BOOKS
A Division of Thomas Nelson Publishers
Since 1798

www.thomasnelson.com

Published in Nashville, Tennessee, by Thomas Nelson, Inc.

Managing Editor: Lila Empson
Manuscript written and prepared by Marcia Ford
Design: Whisner Design Group, Tulsa, Oklahoma

Library of Congress Cataloging-in-Publication Data

Checklist for life for teachers.
    p. cm.
  ISBN 0-7852-6002-1 (pbk.)
  1. Christian teachers—Religious life. I. Thomas Nelson Publishers.
  BV4596.T43.C44 2005
  248.8'8—dc22   2004028652

Heart Attitude

I will ask God to help me set
achievable goals for my life.

Table of Contents

Table of Contents Continued

Introduction

My instruction is far more valuable than silver or gold. For the value of wisdom is far above rubies; nothing can be compared with it. —Proverbs 8:10–11 TLB

Every year, for roughly 180 days, you hold the awesome responsibility of guiding children and youth through their formative years, teaching, training, and leading them as they draw closer to maturity and independence. No matter what grade level you teach, no matter what subject you specialize in, you have dedicated the school year to influencing and instructing young people. And for the remaining 185 days? You're still a teacher, because teaching is not only what you do but is also an integral element of who you are.

As a Christian teacher, you have a great deal more to offer your students than knowledge and skills. You provide your students with a role model; one that you hope and pray is a positive, godly example of right living. And you provide them with biblical wisdom, even if you never quote the Bible, because your character has been formed by the wisdom you have gleaned from the Scriptures. It hardly matters whether you see that or not. They see it, and it matters greatly in their lives.

There's no question that your task is a daunting one. The Bible even acknowledges this: "Don't be in any rush to become a teacher, my friends. Teaching is highly responsible work. Teachers are held to the strictest standards" (James 3:1 THE MESSAGE). Sometimes, the responsibility seems overwhelming, the standards impossible to achieve. But God does not want you to consider your calling an overwhelming impossibility. That's where *Checklist for Life for Teachers* comes in. Drawing on the eternal wisdom of Scripture, each of the following sixty-six devotionals offers inspiration and practical help as you seek to have an impact on the world in a God-honoring way.

Each chapter offers a reflection on a character trait or classroom-related issue that applies the truth of Scripture to everyday experiences. Many of the scenarios are based on actual classroom experiences. The checklists that follow offer you an opportunity to do a "heart" check on your attitudes toward God, your work, and other people, as well as a selection of practical tips to use in your personal life and in the classroom.

Consider the devotionals to be a source of encouragement as you continue in the wonderful calling you are pursuing. May God strengthen you and give you wisdom and joy both in and out of the classroom!

Paul wrote: "Until I come, devote yourself to the public reading of Scripture, to preaching and to teaching."

1 TIMOTHY 4:13 NIV

Have reverence for Christ in your hearts, and honor him as Lord. Be ready at all times to answer anyone who asks you to explain the hope you have in you, but do it with gentleness and respect.

1 PETER 3:15–16 GNT

Paul wrote: "You have heard me teach many things that have been confirmed by many reliable witnesses. Teach these great truths to trustworthy people who are able to pass them on to others."

2 TIMOTHY 2:2 NLT

Paul wrote: "Imitate me, just as I also imitate Christ."

1 CORINTHIANS 11:1 NKJV

A teacher who is attempting to teach without inspiring the pupil with a desire to learn is hammering on a cold iron.

—HORACE MANN

The mediocre teacher tells. The good teacher explains. The superior teacher demonstrates. The great teacher inspires.

—WILLIAM W. WARD

Checklist for Life *for Teachers*

The end of learning is to know God, and out of that knowledge to love Him and imitate Him.

—JOHN MILTON

Passion

Contagious Enthusiasm

Paul wrote: "Be strong and steady, always enthusiastic about the Lord's work, for you know that nothing you do for the Lord is ever useless."

—1 Corinthians 15:58 NLT

Jim Henderson won't soon forget the high-school teacher who inspired him to pursue education as a career. Mrs. Schiavo taught algebra and geometry—required courses for students on a college track. Math was not Jim's strongest subject; after a tough first year, he questioned his ability to pass second-year algebra and go on to college. But several weeks into the new school year Jim realized he was listening better, understanding more, and getting better grades in math as a result.

What made the difference, Jim says, were Mrs. Schiavo and her genuine enthusiasm for her subject and the students she taught. "Look at this!" she'd say excitedly, moving around the room as she showed the students how to solve an equation and opened their eyes to a new way of looking at math. Her energy was so infectious that she pumped new life into Jim's plans for his future, giving him the confidence to believe he, too, could instill a passion for learning in others. Today he is a popular history teacher in a Midwest middle school.

Jim—now Mr. Henderson—realized he could not expect his students to become excited about learning unless he was excited about teaching. From Mrs. Schiavo and others like her, he learned to express his enthusiasm through his facial expressions, voice, gestures, and even his word choices. He moved around the room, maintaining eye contact with students and occasionally doing the unpredictable. The lively classroom interaction that followed mirrored his energetic style.

Start by making little changes in the way you usually conduct yourself in the classroom. If you usually stand in front of the class, start walking around the room more. Add a bit more life to the way you speak. As you're teaching, keep in mind the root meaning of *enthusiasm*—"in God" or "inspired by God." Be "in God" even as you stand before your class, trusting Him to inspire you to present the subject matter in a way that will help your students listen better and understand more.

Think back to those things that factored in to your decision to become a teacher: A passion for a particular subject, a genuine love of young people, a desire to pass on your knowledge and enthusiasm to future generations—and a teacher who modeled all of that for you. Now you have the opportunity to be that kind of teacher to your students. Inject new life into your teaching style by becoming excited once again over those things that first attracted you to the classroom. Enthusiasm—being "in God"—*is* contagious. As a teacher, you have a wonderful, captive audience just waiting to catch it.

I Will

Ask God to renew the passion that first drew
me to teaching.

yes   *no*

Inject new life into my teaching style.

yes   *no*

Remember those teachers whose enthusiasm
stirred up my own and learn from their examples.

yes   *no*

Be thankful for the opportunity to instill a love
of learning in my students.

yes   *no*

Be aware of the things I do that result in a vibrant
learning atmosphere and build on those strengths.

yes   *no*

Believe that my love of teaching will have an
impact on my students.

yes   *no*

Things to Do

☐ *Write down your memories of a teacher you had whose enthusiasm impacted you, paying close attention to details that you could integrate into your teaching style.*

☐ *Imagine yourself as one of your students. Remember how a teacher's passion affected you at that age and complete this thought: "I wish [your name] would . . ."*

☐ *Do something unpredictable—such as become a character or historical person related to your subject and teach as if you were that person. That will catch your students off guard in a positive way and also infuse new life into your teaching routine.*

☐ *Focus on your vocal delivery for the next few days and see if you can inject more liveliness and energy into it.*

☐ *Ask several trusted colleagues to evaluate the enthusiasm you exhibit for teaching. Keep an open mind and pray about their responses.*

Things to Remember

You will go out in joy and be led forth in peace; the mountains and hills will burst into song before you, and all the trees of the field will clap their hands.

ISAIAH 55:12 NIV

Let all those who take refuge and put their trust in You rejoice; let them ever sing and shout for joy, because You make a covering over them and defend them; let those also who love Your name be joyful in You and be in high spirits.

PSALM 5:11 AMP

The psalmist wrote: "I call out at the top of my lungs, 'GOD! Answer! I'll do whatever you say.' "

PSALM 119:145 THE MESSAGE

The LORD said: "For you that honor my name, victory will shine like the sun with healing in its rays, and you will jump about like calves at play."

MALACHI 4:2 CEV

Jesus said: "These things I have spoken to you so that My joy may be in you, and that your joy may be made full."

JOHN 15:11 NASB

With a leap, [a lame man] stood upright and began to walk; and he entered the temple with [Peter and John], walking and leaping and praising God.

ACTS 3:8 NASB

Nothing is so contagious as enthusiasm; it moves stones, it charms brutes.

—EDWARD BULWER-LYTTON

Knowledge is power, but enthusiasm pulls the switch.

—IVERN BALL

Commitment

Total Dedication

Paul wrote: "Until I come, devote yourself to the public reading of Scripture, to preaching and to teaching."
—1 TIMOTHY 4:13 NIV

You've heard the phrase a thousand times or more: "dedicated teacher." Coworkers and parents may have used that very phrase to describe you and your commitment to the lifework you've chosen. In describing you in that way, people are acknowledging your unswerving dedication to that work as well as to the young people you teach. It's among the highest of compliments a teacher can receive.

The word *dedication* itself implies much more than the intention to see a job through to its completion. It signifies wholehearted immersion in the task at hand, a devotion to your mission in life that involves your body, mind, and spirit. It's easy to see why that word came into common use to describe the best teachers, because that's what teaching entails: the involvement of your whole being in the work you do.

There's another definition of dedication, though, that you might not have considered in relation to your job. That's the notion of being set apart or consecrated for a special use. A sacramental item, such as a chalice used during communion in church, is said to be dedicated for that one purpose. In a similar way, you, as a dedicated teacher, have been set apart for a special purpose, the shaping of the lives of the young people. That's a heady assignment, but it's one that you are equal to—because God is the One who has consecrated you for the work you do, as well as the One who gives you the strength to remain dedicated to that work.

One aspect of your dedication to teaching is the lifelong commitment you've made to the profession. But there's also the sense of daily dedication, the ability to live out your commitment in the midst of difficult days and routine schedules and constant challenges. Dedicating each day to God serves as a reminder of your own dedication to your mission and the young people you serve, and strengthens you to follow through on the commitments you've made for that day.

Your wholehearted immersion in your work is not only pleasing to God but also inspiring to your colleagues and your students. Your commitment shows them what it takes to remain faithful to a task for the long haul. You may never see the impact that has on those around you. But you've come to accept that as part of the package of being a teacher. You teach because you are dedicated to fulfilling your mission as a teacher—regardless of the visible, short-term results.

I Will

Continue to dedicate my life to teaching and to serving my students.

yes _____ _no_ _____

See myself as set apart for a special purpose in life.

yes _____ _no_ _____

Commit each day to God.

yes _____ _no_ _____

Follow through on my daily commitments, in my personal life and professional life.

yes _____ _no_ _____

Realize that I may never know the impact my commitment has on others.

yes _____ _no_ _____

Rely on God for the strength to remain faithful to my mission as a teacher.

yes _____ _no_ _____

Things to Do

☐ *Read the book of Acts, paying special attention to the dedication of the early church.*

☐ *Send a note to a teacher from your past whose dedication has inspired you.*

☐ *Read a few chapters of* Foxe's Book of Martyrs *or dc Talk's* Jesus Freaks *to draw inspiration from those whose commitment to God resulted in persecution and death.*

☐ *Set aside one day to recharge your batteries and reflect on your commitment to your job.*

☐ *Create a daily reminder—such as a pop-up note on your computer—that reads: "This day is dedicated to God."*

☐ *Thank a long-time teacher in your school for his or her commitment to teaching and his or her example to other teachers.*

Things to Remember

Because the Lord God helps me, I will not be dismayed; I have set my face like flint to do his will, and I know that I will triumph.

ISAIAH 50:7 TLB

Jesus said: "Which of you, intending to build a tower, does not sit down first and count the cost, whether he has enough to finish it."

LUKE 14:28 NKJV

Be strong and do not lose courage, for there is a reward for your work.

2 CHRONICLES 15:7 NASB

Even though our outer nature suffers decay, our inner self is renewed day after day.

2 CORINTHIANS 4:16 MLB

Jesus said: "Staying with it—that's what God requires. Stay with it to the end. You won't be sorry, and you'll be saved."

MATTHEW 24:13 THE MESSAGE

Commit your works to the LORD, and your plans will be established.

PROVERBS 16:3 NASB

These troubles and sufferings of ours are, after all, quite small and won't last very long. Yet this short time of distress will result in God's richest blessing upon us forever and ever!

2 CORINTHIANS 4:17 TLB

Never doubt that a small group of committed people can change the world.

—MARGARET MEAD

It is a great deal easier to do that which God gives us to do, no matter how hard it is, than to face the responsibilities of not doing it.

—J. R. MILLER

Cheerfulness

Smiling Before Christmas

All the days of the afflicted are evil, but he who is of a merry heart has a continual feast.

—PROVERBS 15:15 NKJV

Teachers who have been in the profession for a while likely remember the advice given years ago to education majors in college: "Never smile before Christmas." The thinking at the time was that you had to maintain a stern demeanor and let your pupils know that you meant business if you expected to maintain order and discipline in the classroom. You could not drop your guard even slightly until some time halfway through the school year, when the students were so used to your strictness that you could afford to smile now and then.

What were those professors thinking? Imagine all of those bright young college students, full of eagerness to teach and affection for children, suddenly being told that they had to ignore their instincts in order to lay down the law. Imagine *you* being told that today. Thankfully, that piece of advice went the way of corporal punishment in the classroom as educational researchers began to realize that children learned best in a loving, nurturing, and cheerful environment. Teachers, of course, knew all along that it's nearly impossible to suppress a smile when you're surrounded all day by some of the funniest and most charming people on the planet, no matter how exasperating they may be at times.

So smile—and keep smiling. Your cheerfulness in the classroom can turn a bad day around for the boy whose home life is in shambles, the girl whose grades are causing her stress, and every other student who just needs to see a smiling face, for whatever reason. And the great thing about it is that you can *decide* to be cheerful, regardless of the circumstances in your own life or the kind of day you are having. Choosing to be cheerful is not a form of deception, either. By *acting* cheerful, you can actually *become* cheerful. You simply set your own problems aside temporarily, resolving to deal with them when you're away from the watchful eyes of the young people who need you to bring a bit of sunshine into their lives.

The Bible says that God loves a cheerful giver. That verse applies to money, but it's probably safe to assume that He's equally pleased when you cheerfully give of yourself in the classroom. Ask Him to help you light up that room by maintaining a pleasant countenance and attitude throughout the day. Put a smile on your face—before, during, and after Christmas.

I Will

Decide to be cheerful. _____ yes _____ no

Realize that my countenance affects my students. _____ yes _____ no

Smile before Christmas. _____ yes _____ no

Thank God for the delightful young people He has placed in my life. _____ yes _____ no

Set aside my own problems when I'm in the presence of my students. _____ yes _____ no

Pray that I will be able to bring some sunshine into others' lives. _____ yes _____ no

Remember to maintain a cheerful attitude around my colleagues as well. _____ yes _____ no

Things to Do

☐ Memorize one of the accompanying Scriptures so you can recall it during the school day.

☐ Place a rubber band around your wrist for one day and snap it—hard—each time you catch yourself acting gloomy; see how quickly you cheer up.

☐ Decorate your classroom to create a sunny, cheerful environment.

☐ Come up with a variety of pleasant responses to unpleasant remarks you're likely to hear at school.

☐ Make a list of the ways you can be more cheerful as a teacher and do the first three immediately (for example, stand by the door and greet students by name as they enter the room—even in high school).

☐ Start a collection of uplifting quotations to use in lessons or post in your classroom.

Things to Remember

Always look happy and cheerful.

ECCLESIASTES 9:8 GNT

Let each one give as he has planned in his heart, neither grudgingly nor by compulsion; for God loves a happy giver.

2 CORINTHIANS 9:7 MLB

Are any of you in trouble? Then you should pray. Are any of you happy? Then sing songs of praise.

JAMES 5:13 NIrV

A joyful heart makes a cheerful face, but when the heart is sad, the spirit is broken.

PROVERBS 15:13 NASB

David wrote: "When I was upset and beside myself, you calmed me down and cheered me up."

PSALM 94:19 THE MESSAGE

Happy are the people who are in such a state; happy are the people whose God is the LORD!

PSALM 144:15 NKJV

It is not fitting, when one is in God's service, to have a gloomy face or a chilling look.
—SAINT FRANCIS OF ASSISI

Let us be of good cheer, knowing that the misfortunes hardest to bear are those which never happen.
—JAMES RUSSELL LOWELL

Courage

Standing Alone

Watch, stand fast in the faith, be brave, be strong.

—1 Corinthians 16:13 NKJV

In your role as a classroom teacher, you are like a commanding officer on the front lines of a battle. Not only do you need to make the tough decisions your position requires, you have to make those decisions in glare of the public spotlight. The troops are looking to you to lead them; the brass are scrutinizing your battlefield judgment; and the public back home is counting on you for the safe return of the young people under your care. The battle? It's for the hearts and minds and future of those young people.

The image of teacher as mighty warrior is not as far-fetched as it may seem. Remember Robin Williams's character in *Dead Poets Society*? He was a private-school English teacher, hardly the kind of person you would imagine in full battle gear. But he stood up, and stood alone among his peers, for what he believed was right, knowing the consequences could be severe.

Look at the apostle Paul: He courageously instructed the leaders of the early church, despite opposition from Rome and

Jerusalem, despite repeated threats to his safety, despite imprisonment. He knew the dangers, but he knew what was right. He never backed down.

But the best example of all is, as always, Jesus. Do you need a bit more confidence that you can make a difference in the classroom and transform your students' lives? Consider the example of Jesus, whose own disciples called Him Teacher: He took a bunch of ordinary guys and transformed them into an exceptional band of brave men who in turn changed the course of history, against all odds.

Are you facing an uphill battle with the administration or the school board? Look at the way Jesus responded to the powerful Roman officials in the final chapters of the Gospels— not with fearful pleadings, but with a courageous silence and a few choice words. And He promises to give you the words you will need: "For it is not you who speak, but the Spirit of your Father who speaks in you" (Matthew 10:20 NKJV).

Most of the situations you face aren't quite that dramatic. Many teachers get the jitters on the first day of school each fall, even after years in the classroom—and for some, the first-day jitters last for weeks. And meeting with the parents of a difficult or struggling student is not for the faint of heart. Neither is handing out a failing grade to a student you wanted so much to pass.

Sometimes, all it takes to muster up the courage you need is a simple reminder of who you are and what you are called to be. Your classroom is the perfect setting for a few strategically placed reminders: a quotation about courage that is especially meaningful to you, positioned on the back wall in your line of vision; a photo or print of someone whose courage has inspired you, also placed where you can see it often; or even something whimsical like a Mighty Mouse figurine or Superman poster, anything that will make you smile at the thought of the courage hidden inside of you. (Your students may wonder about you, but that's okay. They'll see your fun side.)

Your mission as a teacher is a critical one. You hold the future in your hands each time you stand in front of a classroom filled with young people, some eager, some unmotivated, some willing to do what's required of them, some who are there only because they have to be—just like an army unit. But remember, you are all on the same side, and they are all looking to you to lead them, even the ones who are hiding behind their textbooks or seem to look at everything in the room but you.

Ask God for the courage you need to fulfill your mission. Depend on Him to strengthen you and give you confidence to do the right thing, despite any opposition, despite any consequences, despite any fears. He will be standing with you even if you feel that you are standing alone. Thank Him for the many times He has given you courage in the past. Remember, too, to thank Him in advance for the all those times to come when you will need an extra measure of courage.

I Will

Expect God to help me be victorious in my daily battles.

yes   _no_

Learn to stand alone when necessary, knowing God is always with me.

yes   _no_

Stand with others in support of a godly cause.

yes   _no_

Remember the many times God has given me courage in the past.

yes   _no_

See myself as one made in the image of God.

yes   _no_

Recognize fear as a stepping-stone to acting courageously in God's strength.

yes   _no_

Things to Do

 Write out the quote on page 33 from Ambrose Redmoon and post it prominently in your classroom.

Read an inspiring book (Parker Palmer's Courage to Teach, _for example) or journal article that strengthens your courage._

Go to your classroom early one day this week and silently ask God to reinforce the image of you as a brave frontline commander.

Reflect on a time when you acted courageously as a teacher and write about it in your journal.

Memorize one or more of the Scriptures on the next two pages, asking God to bring them to mind when you need them.

Offer your support to a colleague who needs an extra measure of courage right now.

Things to Remember

Paul wrote: "We overwhelmingly conquer through Him who loved us."

ROMANS 8:37 NASB

Do not throw away this confident trust in the Lord, no matter what happens. Remember the great reward it brings you!

HEBREWS 10:35 NLT

Be very courageous to keep and to do all that is written in the Book of the Law of Moses, lest you turn aside from it to the right hand or to the left.
Joshua 23:6 NKJV

The wicked run away when no one is chasing them, but the godly are as bold as lions.

PROVERBS 28:1 NLT

Be of good courage, and He shall strengthen your heart, all you who hope in the LORD.

PSALM 31:24 NKJV

Moses said: "He is my God, and I will praise Him; my father's God, and I will exalt Him."

EXODUS 15:2 NKJV

God said to Joshua: "Be strong and very brave. Make sure you obey the whole law my servant Moses gave you. Do not turn away from it to the right or the left. Then you will have success everywhere you go."

JOSHUA 1:7 NIrV

We can go to God with bold confidence through faith in Christ.

EPHESIANS 3:12 GOD'S WORD

The LORD will be your confidence and will keep your foot from being caught.

PROVERBS 3:26 NASB

David wrote: "Wait on the LORD; be of good courage, and He shall strengthen your heart; wait, I say, on the LORD!"

PSALM 27:14 NKJV

Be of good courage, and let us be strong for our people and for the cities of our God. And may the LORD do what is good in His sight.

1 CHRONICLES 19:13 NKJV

Shechaniah said to Ezra: "Arise, for this matter is your responsibility. We also are with you. Be of good courage, and do it."

EZRA 10:4 NKJV

Courage is not the absence of fear but the judgment that something else is more important than fear.

—AMBROSE REDMOON

Courage is doing what you're afraid to do. There can be no courage unless you're scared.

—EDDIE RICKENBACKER

Excellence

All A's

That you may approve the things that are excellent, that you may be sincere and without offense till the day of Christ.

—PHILIPPIANS 1:10 NKJV

Imagine what teaching would be like if faculty members were to receive report cards as often as their students do. Some teachers might experience the same trepidation their students feel: *What if I flunk?* Others might not be a bit worried, confident that they'll pass muster. One thing is for certain: If you strive for excellence, just as you encourage your students to do, you're likely to see a column of straight A's on *your* report card.

Striving for excellence means doing the best you possibly can with your God-given talent and gifts and abilities. That's the beauty of it: You don't have to work miracles or achieve perfection or live up to the unrealistic expectations of others. Pursuing excellence is a lifelong process that you live out daily. You try to do your best each day, and even though some days you will be more successful than others, you can still rest your head on your pillow at night knowing you gave it your all.

Individuals excel in ways that are unique to them. But to be considered excellent at who they are and what they do, people must exhibit certain common characteristics, such as being men and women of high moral character.

The same is true of different professions; excellent teachers don't see their students as just *teenagers*, for example, with the loaded connotations that word implies; they see them as Jason and Megan and Michael. They continually improve their teaching skills by innovating and taking risks and learning from other teachers.

First and foremost in the minds of excellent teachers is concern for the students and how those students are affected by everything they do, both in and out of the classroom. A shortcut that shortchanges the students is never worth it to the best teachers—but they're quick to take advantage of those blessed shortcuts that benefit the students. They carry their heavy responsibilities lightly, allowing God to take their burdens so their students will never feel as if *they* were the burden.

Pursuing excellence affects all areas of your life, not just the classroom. Make sure you apply the test of excellence in your home life, your relationships, and your church and community involvement. In a sense, excellence is doing what should come naturally to you as a child of God: relying on Him to help you make the best of everything He has placed within you, all the while aiming for straight A's.

I Will

Pursue excellence each day.   yes ___   no ___

Understand that my students are also affected by
who I am and what I do outside the classroom.   yes ___   no ___

Recognize and build on my God-given talents,
gifts, and abilities.   yes ___   no ___

Be a person of high moral character.   yes ___   no ___

Pray that God will enable me to make the best of
all He has placed within me.   yes ___   no ___

Model excellence by never shortchanging my
students by taking the easy way out.   yes ___   no ___

Realize that achieving excellence is a lifelong pursuit. ___   yes ___   no ___

Things to Do

☐ Grade yourself on some of the parenthesized topics in the Table of
Contents, such as honesty, patience, and cheerfulness. Make a note to
do this again in three months to gauge your improvement.

☐ Write in your journal about the ways you already "autograph your work
with excellence," as the author of the accompanying quotation advised.

☐ Ask God to show you specific ways you can strive for excellence in your
body, mind, and spirit.

☐ Create an age-appropriate poster or bulletin board display showing that
when excellence is the goal, better grades follow.

☐ Read 1 Corinthians 13 to discover what the apostle Paul described as
"the most excellent way."

☐ Meditate on how you can "excel in living a God-pleasing life even more
than you already do" (1 Thessalonians 4:1 GOD'S WORD).

Things to Remember

Paul wrote: "Eagerly desire the greater gifts. And now I will show you the most excellent way."

1 CORINTHIANS 12:31 NIV

Since you are eager for spiritual gifts, seek to excel in the upbuilding of the church.

1 CORINTHIANS 14:12 MLB

Wisdom cries out: "Hear; for I will speak of excellent things; and the opening of my lips shall be right things."

PROVERBS 8:6 KJV

O LORD our Lord, how excellent is thy name in all the earth! who hast set thy glory above the heavens.

PSALM 8:1 KJV

Know His will, and approve the things that are excellent, being instructed out of the law.

ROMANS 2:18 NKJV

Paul wrote: "Now then, brothers and sisters, because of the Lord Jesus we ask and encourage you to excel in living a God-pleasing life even more than you already do. Do this the way we taught you."

1 THESSALONIANS 4:1 GOD'S WORD

Excellence is a self-portrait of the person who did it. Autograph your work with excellence.

—AUTHOR UNKNOWN

All excellent things are as difficult as they are rare.

—BENEDICT SPINOZA

Delegating Responsibility

May I Have a Volunteer?

Both you and these people who are with you will surely wear yourselves out. For this thing is too much for you; you are not able to perform it by yourself.

—EXODUS 18:18 NKJV

Like many first-year teachers, Mr. Lawson quickly found his workload to be overwhelming. Paperwork to complete, lessons to plan, papers to grade, a classroom to maintain—those needed immediate attention and left little time for important things like getting to know the students. What's more, his wife and newborn needed him, but concerns about school often distracted him when he was at home. He didn't want to appear inadequate, so instead of seeking help he continued to do everything himself.

That's when an experienced and compassionate colleague stepped in. Mrs. Hamilton always kept an eye out for those teachers—especially novices—who were likely candidates for burnout. After telling Mr. Lawson about her own burnout years earlier, she offered a wealth of practical advice and information: a list of tasks he could turn over to aides and office staff; streamlined methods for handling routine chores; a much-needed primer on the willingness of students to help. She proved to be the godsend he so desperately needed.

Like Mr. Lawson, you have many demands on your life. It doesn't matter whether you're a novice or a veteran: You need to find ways to deal with those demands effectively. You will not appear to be inadequate; on the contrary, your decision to handle what is clearly a problem will reflect well on your ability to find solutions.

So what can you do? First, recognize how eager some students are to assist teachers. Seek volunteers to run errands on campus (depending on school policy, of course) or keep the classroom orderly and aesthetically pleasing. Second, look to your colleagues. If you're new to teaching or to a particular school, find someone who knows the drill and ask for insider information on how much and what type of work can realistically be delegated to aides and support staff. Even if you're a seasoned veteran, you probably know someone who seems to have a handle on how to get others to help. And don't forget the parents. Many are ready to help out in whatever way they can.

If you don't stop and reflect on your life—and take appropriate action—you will surely wear yourself out. This "thing"—the responsibility you bear—may well be too much for you. Ask God to guide you in determining how to delegate responsibility to others. And be prepared to rediscover the energy and enthusiasm you started out with.

I Will

Stay connected with God daily.

yes _____ no _____

Learn to delegate more of the tasks in my life.

yes _____ no _____

Rely on God to help me sort out my responsibilities.

yes _____ no _____

Learn to cut back when my obligations become
overwhelming.

yes _____ no _____

Be on the lookout for streamlined procedures in
the classroom.

yes _____ no _____

Share helpful "insider information" with
other teachers.

yes _____ no _____

Accept the fact that I cannot do it all alone.

yes _____ no _____

Things to Do

☐ *Give students an opportunity to help you with routine classroom chores, offering an age-appropriate incentive if necessary.*

☐ *Strategize with a colleague on the best ways to enlist the support of others.*

☐ *Create a phone/e-mail list of reliable parent volunteers and let them know how they can assist you.*

☐ *Subscribe to one of the many print or online magazines for teachers, which frequently offer tips on streamlining tasks.*

☐ *Take a novice under your wing—or if you are a novice, ask a veteran for advice.*

☐ *Join an Internet discussion group for teachers and seek help with a specific challenge, such as dealing with paperwork.*

Things to Remember

May the God of peace Himself sanctify you completely; and may your whole spirit, soul, and body be preserved blameless at the coming of our Lord Jesus Christ.

1 THESSALONIANS 5:23 NKJV

Jesus said: "Take care to live in me, and let me live in you. For a branch can't produce fruit when severed from the vine. Nor can you be fruitful apart from me."

JOHN 15:4 TLB

Let all things be done decently and in order.

1 CORINTHIANS 14:40 NKJV

Let your moderation be known unto all men. The Lord is at hand.

PHILIPPIANS 4:5 KJV

Jesus answered and said to her, "Martha, Martha, you are worried and troubled about many things. But one thing is needed, and Mary has chosen that good part, which will not be taken away from her."

LUKE 10:41–42 NKJV

Paul wrote: "Though I am absent in the flesh, yet I am with you in spirit, rejoicing to see your good order and the steadfastness of your faith in Christ."

COLOSSIANS 2:5 NKJV

> **Surround yourself with the best people you can find, delegate authority, and don't interfere.**
> —RONALD REAGAN

> **Delegating works, providing the one delegating works too.**
> —ROBERT HALF

Accountability

Open Admission

Each of us will give an account of himself to God.
—ROMANS 14:12 NIV

Sarah Anderson was brought up short as she read the newspaper after a long day in the classroom. Three teachers had been charged with helping students a bit too much on a standardized test—one whose results would determine how much state money the district would get the following year. Eager to show that the students' test scores had improved—the criterion used to determine the funding—the teachers suggested that students "try again" whenever they discovered a wrong answer as they walked around the room.

Horrified, Mrs. Anderson recalled that same temptation occurring to her on test day at her school. In fact, had she not been distracted by a student who had become ill during the test, she wondered if she would have encouraged certain students to look over certain answers a bit more carefully. Like every other teacher in the state, she knew how much was riding on the test results. And now she realized the temptation she felt was not at all unusual.

That did it. For three years, her husband had faithfully met with an accountability partner at the suggestion of their pastor. Weekly he shared with her his victories over temptation, sometimes in detail, often in general. She had longed for a similar relationship with another teacher but kept putting it off. But no longer. Within minutes she was on the phone to a faithful friend and colleague, asking if she would be her accountability partner. The friend agreed.

From her husband, Mrs. Anderson had learned the drill: Meet regularly with someone you trust completely. Maintain absolute confidentiality. Begin and end your time together in prayer, asking God to keep both of you vulnerable and honest, enable you to speak the truth in love, and give you the grace to rebuke when necessary and forgive without hesitation. Share the general areas in your life in which you are most susceptible to the temptation to sin. Then confess your sins, being specific and avoiding superficiality. Instead of "I need to be more loving," admit "I simply cannot muster up one bit of love for that Hoffman kid." And remember to celebrate your victories.

Being accountable to others, of course, is no substitute for accountability to God. The two go hand in hand. You need to be just as open and honest and vulnerable to God as you are to another human being. Maintain daily contact with Him, in order to keep your accounts short and draw on His power to resist temptation and His grace to walk in forgiveness. He's the best accountability partner you could ever ask for.

I Will

Be accountable to at least one other person.

   yes   *no*

Be open and vulnerable with my accountability partner.

   yes   *no*

Maintain total confidentiality regarding what is shared in our sessions.

   yes   *no*

Make sure my confession is specific and truthful.

   yes   *no*

Daily confess my sins to God and draw on His strength to resist temptation.

   yes   *no*

Accept rebuke with grace.

   yes   *no*

Ask God to enable me to speak the truth in love to my accountability partner.

   yes   *no*

Things to Do

 Find an accountability partner who shares your faith and set up a regular schedule for sessions together.

☐ *Start an accountability notebook. Jot down what you need to discuss before you meet, and take notes during your sessions.*

☐ *Make your partner aware of the general areas of weakness in which you are most vulnerable (thought life, sexual temptation, sins of the tongue) before you confess details.*

☐ *For each vulnerable area in your life, list specific things you can start doing to avoid temptation.*

☐ *Memorize Galatians 6:1 and Romans 14:12 as a reminder to be accountable to others as well as to God.*

☐ *Spend some time explaining accountability to your students—what it is, whom they are accountable to, and what they are accountable for.*

Things to Remember

If someone is caught in any kind of wrongdoing, those of you who are spiritual should set him right; but you must do it in a gentle way. And keep an eye on yourselves, so that you will not be tempted, too.

GALATIANS 6:1 GNT

Confess your sins to one another, and pray for one another so that you may be healed. The effective prayer of a righteous man can accomplish much.

JAMES 5:16 NASB

Job said: "What answer would I give to God when he judges me?"

JOB 31:14 CEV

Jesus said: "Here is what I tell you. On judgment day, people will have to account for every careless word they have spoken."

MATTHEW 12:36 NIrV

Why does the wicked man revile God? Why does he say to himself, "He won't call me to account?"

PSALM 10:13 NIV

We know that whatever the Law says, it speaks to those who are under the Law, so that [the murmurs and excuses of] every mouth may be hushed and all the world may be held accountable to God.

ROMANS 3:19 AMP

Life is not accountable to us. We are accountable to life.

—DENIS WAITLEY

It is not only what we do but what we do not do for which we are accountable.

—JEAN-BAPTISTE MOLIÉRE

Patience

Counting to Ten

We show we are servants of God by our pure lives, our understanding, patience, and kindness, by the Holy Spirit, by true love.

—2 CORINTHIANS 6:6 NCV

From the first day Jeremy entered Miss Ferguson's classroom, the fourth-grade teacher knew she would be facing a significant challenge. As a new student in a small, rural school, Jeremy—who had lived in L.A. all of his life—seemed to need a great deal of personal attention as he adjusted to the unfamiliar environment. Chalking his problems up to the newness of the situation, Miss Ferguson took a lot of deep breaths as she slowed down her normal teaching pace and patiently worked with him.

What she didn't know was that Jeremy had been categorized as learning disabled in his previous school. There was no mention of it in the file she had been given, and it wasn't until the end of the school year that she discovered what would seem to be a crucial bit of information about his background. But a funny thing happened despite the school system's failure to notify her: Jeremy had made significant progress that year.

Miss Ferguson doesn't know if Jeremy's former school district had incorrectly identified him as learning disabled or whether he simply managed to overcome his disability. But she does believe his improvement can be attributed in part to the way she chose to handle what she thought was an adjustment problem. By being patient with Jeremy and allowing him to work at his own pace, Miss Ferguson unknowingly helped him avoid being inappropriately labeled for the rest of his school years—and she brought him up to speed simply by slowing down.

People often joke about asking God to give them patience—*now!* Certainly, God can help you to be more patient and understanding with others. But the truth is, He has already given you that ability. What you may need is a bit of discipline and a few helpful reminders about what it takes to nurture the quality of patience.

First of all, pray—and then slow down. That may seem like a tall order. A typical school day is hardly conducive to maintaining a leisurely pace. But leisure doesn't figure in to it at all. Your mind can still be actively engaged as you downshift and give your attention to the matter at hand—whether it's a challenging student, a chaotic discipline problem, or a difficult administrator.

Concentrate on keeping your composure. The last thing you want to do as a teacher is to lose it—whether that means your temper or your cool or your very last nerve. God's Spirit can envelop you with His peace and empower you to maintain your self-control.

One of the reasons people lose their patience with others is that they fail to take into account the many distinctions in the way people react and respond and think and make decisions—and learn. If you expect students to generally learn according to any one of a dozen known methods, it's going to take an extra measure of patience to adjust to that one student who seems to learn best according to a thirteenth—and untested—method.

The same holds true in your interactions with your colleagues, who can sometimes test your patience more than your students do. Keep in mind that every administrator and every other teacher has pressures and life challenges that extend far beyond the campus—just as you do. You have the opportunity, as a child of God, to cut them some slack and give them the gift of your patient understanding, whether or not they ever return the favor.

Finally, let go of the things you cannot control, such as coworkers who disrupt your day, parents who consume your time, and the demands of a bureaucracy whose love of forms seems to have no end. It's not worth losing your patience over matters that are out of your hands. Pray for the grace to endure the situation with serenity and a good attitude.

Like Miss Ferguson, you may not always realize the effect your attitude is having on those around you at the time. Your patient attention may be exactly what one child needs to get over the hump that is keeping him from succeeding in school. Or it could make all the difference in a stressed-out colleague's day. One thing is certain: Cultivating patience will make a difference in *your* day—and in your life.

I Will

Ask God to give me the grace to be patient with others.

yes _____ no _____

Learn to slow down when I begin to feel impatient.

yes _____ no _____

Practice giving my full attention to the challenge at hand, no matter how frustrating it is.

yes _____ no _____

Be as patient with my colleagues as I am with my students.

yes _____ no _____

Let go of things I cannot control.

yes _____ no _____

Take individual ways of responding into account in my interactions with others.

yes _____ no _____

Things to Do

 Come up with three creative ways to handle the student who tests your patience the most.

Choose one of the accompanying Scriptures to memorize.

Create a time-out ritual for yourself—something you can do during the school day when you need to regain your composure.

Discuss with several colleagues practical ways to maintain your patience in the classroom.

Develop a specific strategy for responding to those students who are particularly skilled at pushing your impatience button.

Look up references to God's patience in a concordance or topical Bible (or online) and thank Him for how patient He is with His creation.

Make a list of those things you try to control but have no control over—and let go of them.

Things to Remember

The Lord isn't really being slow about his promise to return, as some people think. No, he is being patient for your sake. He does not want anyone to perish, so he is giving more time for everyone to repent.

2 PETER 3:9 NLT

Always be humble, gentle, and patient, accepting each other in love.

EPHESIANS 4:2 NCV

The end of a thing is better than its beginning; the patient in spirit is better than the proud in spirit.
Ecclesiastes 7:8 NKJV

After waiting patiently, Abraham received what was promised.

HEBREWS 6:15 NIV

James wrote: "Be patient, then, my friends, until the Lord comes. See how patient farmers are as they wait for their land to produce precious crops. They wait patiently for the autumn and spring rains."

JAMES 5:7 GNT

Jesus said: "By your steadfastness and patient endurance you shall win the true life of your souls."

LUKE 21:19 AMP

For many years You had patience with them, and testified against them by Your Spirit in Your prophets. Yet they would not listen; therefore You gave them into the hand of the peoples of the lands.

NEHEMIAH 9:30 NKJV

You also must be patient. Establish your hearts [strengthen and confirm them in the final certainty], for the coming of the Lord is very near.

JAMES 5:8 AMP

A hot-tempered man stirs up dissension, but a patient man calms a quarrel.

PROVERBS 15:18 NIV

Be patient and trust the LORD. Don't let it bother you when all goes well for those who do sinful things.

PSALM 37:7 CEV

David wrote: "I waited patiently for the LORD; and He inclined to me, and heard my cry."

PSALM 40:1 NKJV

Be glad for all God is planning for you. Be patient in trouble, and always be prayerful.

ROMANS 12:12 NLT

Patient waiting is often the highest way of doing God's will.

—JEREMY COLLIER

He who waits on God never waits too long.

—CHUCK WAGNER

Selflessness

Thinking of Others

Let no one seek his own, but each one the other's well-being.

—1 CORINTHIANS 10:24 NKJV

When people hear the word *selfless,* they most likely think of a great religious figure like Billy Graham or the late Mother Teresa. But countless parents know that some of the most selfless people in the world are the women and men who give of themselves every day in the classroom. Teachers who are committed to their students and their profession spend their lives imparting what they know and who they are to generations of young people who will carry everything they've received from their teachers into the future. That may not be on your mind as you are in the middle of a lesson, but that is the dynamic that's taking place.

You probably don't think of yourself as selfless and might even feel embarrassed to have that description applied to you. That's to be expected, because to be selfless means to turn the attention away from you and on to other people. It means placing a low priority on your own self-interest, thinking more about others, and taking care of their needs first. It involves investing yourself in the lives of others—something you do without consciously thinking about it, day in and day out, all through the school year.

There's also a deeper aspect of selflessness, one that was demonstrated by the most selfless person who ever lived—Jesus—when He traded the perfection of heaven for the limitations of earth to redeem humanity from the ravages and penalty of sin. He was rejected by religious and political leaders, denied by one of His disciples, betrayed by another, condemned to death, tortured, mocked, and abandoned by His friends at the cross. And He did all of this for no personal gain whatsoever. He endured pain and degradation for the sake of every person on earth—including you. He died so you may live.

Jesus' actions made it clear that the deeper aspect of selflessness means dying to your own interests for the sake of others. When you experience a transformation that is that profound, living for others seems like the only way to live. The tendency toward selfishness is a strong one, however, and you need to draw on the power of God's Spirit to continue living for others. But even when you think you've failed—when it seems your selfish thoughts have taken over—your daily commitment to the students in your care demonstrates otherwise.

I Will

Invest my life in the lives of my students.   *yes*   *no*

Consider the needs of others before my own.   *yes*   *no*

Place a low priority on my self-interests.   *yes*   *no*

Realize that the tendency toward selfishness is a powerful one.   *yes*   *no*

Rely on God's Spirit to enable me to live for others.   *yes*   *no*

Apply the principles of Jesus' selflessness to my relationship with my students.   *yes*   *no*

Resist the tendency to place my own interests above others'.   *yes*   *no*

Things to Do

☐ *Read about Jesus' selflessness in Luke 9:18–27.*

☐ *Volunteer for a needed task at school that no other teacher wants to do.*

☐ *Meditate on what it means to exchange your old self for a new identity in Christ.*

☐ *Read a brief biography of Mother Teresa, who became a twentieth-century symbol of selflessness.*

☐ *See how long you can go without saying the word* I.

☐ *Give up a favorite activity this week and spend that time praying for others or doing a favor for someone else.*

☐ *Memorize one or more of the accompanying Scriptures.*

Things to Remember

[Love] does not behave rudely, does not seek its own, is not provoked, thinks no evil.

1 CORINTHIANS 13:5 NKJV

If a brother or sister is naked and destitute of daily food, and one of you says to them, "Depart in peace, be warmed and filled," but you do not give them the things which are needed for the body, what does it profit?

JAMES 2:15–16 NKJV

Love your enemies and do good to them; lend and expect nothing back. You will then have a great reward, and you will be children of the Most High God. For he is good to the ungrateful and the wicked.

LUKE 6:35 GNT

Paul wrote: "I have no one else like Timothy, who truly cares for you. Other people are interested only in their own lives, not in the work of Jesus Christ."

PHILIPPIANS 2:20–21 NCV

Let nothing be done through selfish ambition or conceit, but in lowliness of mind let each esteem others better than himself.

PHILIPPIANS 2:3 NKJV

If you take little account of yourself, you will have peace, wherever you live.

—ABBA POEMEN

As a man goes down in self, he goes up in God.

—GEORGE B. CHEEVER

Pride

Preventive Measure

First pride, then the crash—the bigger the ego,
the harder the fall.

—Proverbs 16:18 THE MESSAGE

You've heard the expression "Pride goes before a fall." This popular rendition comes from the Bible: "Pride goes before destruction, and a haughty spirit before a fall" (Proverbs 16:18 NKJV). You've probably seen it played out in real life: arrogant, corrupt officials who think they're above the law but end up in prison, self-righteous moralists who get caught with their hands in the cookie jar, self-important colleagues who receive poor evaluations. Admit it—it's hard not to feel some measure of satisfaction when those things happen. After all, they got what they deserved. If they hadn't had such a prideful attitude, you might feel more empathy for them.

The problem is that everyone is susceptible to pride— even you. It sneaks up so subtly that you may not even realize it has become a part of your nature. Your spouse says you never really listen anymore; a mother calls to say her child complains that you don't really hear what he's trying to tell you; your last evaluation shows that you seem resistant to suggestions for improvement. If you dig your heels in and refuse to heed these calls for correction, that's a fairly good indication that the sin of pride has worked its way into your life.

Pride manifests itself in other ways, too, like attaching far too much importance to things like your accomplishments, your position in your school, church, or community, or even your appearance. You can ward off the infiltration of these kinds of pride by recognizing the hand others had in all those great things you accomplished, placing more importance on character than status, and giving God the credit for the looks He gave you.

Once you recognize pride and resolve to deal with it, you can overcome a prideful attitude. The first step is to confess your pride to God and ask Him to replace it with a spirit of humility. Admit your error to those who have brought it to your attention and resolve to correct it. Then act on that resolve by taking practical steps to make the changes necessary to correct the situation.

It's hard to be prideful when you're focused on God and other people—and when you're open to correction about yourself. Ask God to soften any hardened edges in your life, places where you've failed to acknowledge your shortcomings or your debt to others or the awesome way God has worked in your life. Don't set yourself up for a fall. Keep pride at bay with a healthy dose of humility.

I Will

Confess the sin of pride to God.   _yes_   _no_

Remain open to correction.   _yes_   _no_

Acknowledge the role others have played in my
success.   _yes_   _no_

Place a greater emphasis on character than
on status.   _yes_   _no_

Ask God to give me a spirit of humility.   _yes_   _no_

Become more other-centered than self-centered.   _yes_   _no_

Believe that God can soften the hardened edges
of my life.   _yes_   _no_

Things to Do

 Think of a recent accomplishment and thank all those who helped you achieve it.

 Dig out your last teacher evaluation, read it with an open mind, and decide how to change those areas that need improvement.

☐ *List the criticisms parents may have made about your teaching style and create a strategy to address their concerns.*

☐ *Read Daniel 4 to find out what happened to Nebuchadnezzar when he allowed pride to take over in his life.*

☐ *Ask your accountability partner to point out any prideful blind spots you may have.*

☐ *Look up* pride *using an online concordance (www.gospelcom.net; www.crosswalk.com) to see how serious God considers this sin to be.*

Things to Remember

Accept correction, and you will find life; reject correction, and you will miss the road.

PROVERBS 10:17 CEV

Let him who thinks he stands take heed lest he fall.

1 CORINTHIANS 10:12 NKJV

Daniel said of Nebuchadnezzar: "When his heart became arrogant and hardened with pride, he was deposed from his royal throne and stripped of his glory."

DANIEL 5:20 NIV

He who keeps instruction is in the way of life, but he who refuses correction goes astray.

PROVERBS 10:17 NKJV

The wicked in his proud countenance does not seek God; God is in none of his thoughts.

PSALM 10:4 NKJV

David wrote: "I'm on the level with you, GOD; I bless you every chance I get."

PSALM 26:12 THE MESSAGE

Pride is tasteless, colorless, and sizeless. Yet it is the hardest thing to swallow.

—AUGUST B. BLACK

God sends no one away empty except those who are full of themselves.

—DWIGHT L. MOODY

Communication

Real-World Language Arts

Walk in wisdom toward those who are outside, redeeming the time. Let your speech always be with grace, seasoned with salt, that you may know how you ought to answer each one.

—COLOSSIANS 4:5–6 NKJV

The members of the Jones County Board of Education could hardly believe their good fortune—the résumé of a highly qualified biology teacher arrived at their office not long after that position unexpectedly became available. They quickly checked out Mr. Carroll's credentials, amassed a file of reference letters, and researched his background. Confident that they had found the ideal person for the position, they invited Mr. Carroll to come in for what they assumed would be a series of interviews.

Mr. Carroll turned out to be a personable young man. He had the demeanor his interviewers liked to see in a classroom teacher, he expressed fondness for the middle-schoolers he would be teaching, and he demonstrated a thorough understanding of the challenges and demands of working in the overcrowded school he would be assigned to. The candidate review committee asked him to return for a second interview the following week.

Later that day, an overnight delivery service arrived with a package and an apology—the delivery had been delayed for several days due to a glitch in the system. The package contained a videotape Mr. Carroll had made of several of his classes in his previous school.

As the tape played on the TV screen, it was all the board members could do to stay awake. After observing three of Mr. Carroll's forty-five-minute classes, they unanimously decided that despite the urgency of the situation, they could not hire this candidate. As brilliant as he was, he failed to communicate with the students. There was no sense of connection between him and the class—or between the material and real life. He had a head full of knowledge but no understanding of how to impart it to others.

For teachers, good communication skills are critical in situations both in and out of the classroom. Think of all the ways you need to communicate in addition to presenting the lessons: explaining procedures and assignments to students, keeping parents and guardians aware of student progress and expectations, soliciting volunteer help in the classroom and on special projects, interacting with other teachers and administrators, submitting reports, leaving instructions for substitute teachers—the list seems endless. Without clear communication, the opportunities for confusion, frustration, and misunderstanding also seem endless.

Becoming a skilled communicator involves placing a set of skills in action. Be concise. Give clear directions. Avoid educational or subject-specific jargon. Have students repeat instructions. Show as well as tell. Use concrete examples. Ask questions effectively; wait for answers, even though the silence that may result can be disconcerting. Think out loud as a means of stimulating discussion. Use creative forms of communicating—auditory, visual, and kinesthetic. Remove the barriers between the classroom and real life by showing students how the subject matter applies to daily living.

Learn the techniques of effective written communication. Keep parents and guardians informed about what you expect of your students, remembering that a bulleted list is more likely to be read than a dense paragraph of prose. Respond to parents' e-mails and phone calls. Follow up on the concerns they voice.

There's a good reason why writing, grammar, and reading have come to be called "language arts"—there's an art to good communication, and for the most part, it's an art that can be learned. In another sense, the ability to communicate well is something God has placed within you. The way you use that ability is important to Him; He wants you to guard your speech, making sure the words you use are accurate and edifying to others. He wants you to avoid saying hurtful things. And He wants you to use your voice to sing His praises.

Ask God to help you become a better communicator, in your speech and in your writing. He is the One who invented speech, and He is the One who best knows how to use it effectively. You cannot find a better language arts teacher.

I Will

Clearly communicate both the lesson material and
any directions to my students. _yes_ _no_

Respond quickly to e-mails, phone messages, and
other communication from parents. _yes_ _no_

Make sure I'm connecting with my students by
gauging their responsiveness to my instruction. _yes_ _no_

Remember to apply each lesson to everyday life. _yes_ _no_

Improve my writing skills. _yes_ _no_

Strive for accuracy in all my communication. _yes_ _no_

Things to Do

☐ *Write an encouraging open letter to your students. Include the date of the next pop quiz or details on an easy extra-credit project in the middle.*

☐ *Resolve to keep "lecture" segments to a minimum, using your students' age as a guideline—for example, eight minutes for eight-year-olds, fifteen minutes for fifteen-year-olds.*

☐ *Create a simple newsletter format for keeping in touch with parents and guardians; schedule periodic deadlines in your lesson book.*

☐ *Videotape the class at different times during a typical day. Analyze your ability to connect with the students, based on their reactions to the lessons.*

☐ *Read (or reread) Strunk and White's* The Elements of Style *to brush up on your writing skills.*

☐ *Find the last extensive memo (or report) you wrote, highlight the jargon, and replace it with commonly used words.*

Things to Remember

Guard what was committed to your trust, avoiding the profane and idle babblings and contradictions of what is falsely called knowledge.

1 Timothy 6:20 NKJV

In Him we live and move and exist, as even some of your own poets have said, "For we also are His children."

Acts 17:28 NASB

✓ *With Jesus' help, let us continually offer our sacrifice of praise to God by proclaiming the glory of his name.*
Hebrews 13:15 NLT

For everything, absolutely everything, above and below, visible and invisible, rank after rank after rank of angels—everything got started in him and finds its purpose in him.

Colossians 1:16 THE MESSAGE

Put away and rid yourselves [completely] of all these things: anger, rage, bad feeling toward others, curses and slander, and foulmouthed abuse and shameful utterances from your lips!

Colossians 3:8 AMP

Let no corrupt word proceed out of your mouth, but what is good for necessary edification, that it may impart grace to the hearers.

Ephesians 4:29 NKJV

Let him that is taught in the word communicate unto him that teacheth in all good things.

GALATIANS 6:6 KJV

Speak an accurate message that cannot be condemned. Then those who oppose us will be ashamed because they cannot say anything bad about us.

TITUS 2:8 GOD'S WORD

Brothers and sisters, think about the things that are good and worthy of praise. Think about the things that are true and honorable and right and pure and beautiful and respected.

PHILIPPIANS 4:8 NCV

Righteous lips are the delight of kings, and they love him who speaks what is right.

PROVERBS 16:13 NKJV

David wrote: "In the assembly of all your people, Lord, I told the good news that you save us. You know that I will never stop telling it."

PSALM 40:9 GNT

The psalmist wrote: "My heart is overflowing with a good theme; I recite my composition concerning the King; my tongue is the pen of a ready writer."

PSALM 45:1 NKJV

Not only to say the right thing in the right place, but far more difficult, to leave unsaid the wrong thing at the tempting moment.

—GEORGE SALA

Information is giving out; communication is getting through.

—SYDNEY J. HARRIS

Fear

Comforting Presence

We may boldly say: "The LORD is my helper; I will not fear. What can man do to me?"

—HEBREWS 13:6 NKJV

Lisa Hamilton had always been known to act like a kid in a candy store each time December rolled around. She loved Christmas, with its bright lights and festive atmosphere and symbolic reminders of the birth of Christ. But in recent years, she had come to dread one aspect of the "holiday season," as it was called in the public elementary school where she taught music. She felt pressured to teach the children songs like "Frosty the Snowman" and "Here Comes Santa Claus" instead of the traditional carols she favored.

"Why don't you just ask if it would be all right to mix in a few carols with the other songs?" a friend at church once asked.

"Oh, you don't understand," she replied. "They'd never let me, and I'm afraid they'd brand me as some kind of troublemaker." It was years before Mrs. Hamilton discovered that her fears were unfounded. The courts had long since determined that teaching traditional carols was legal and acceptable in public schools. Mrs. Hamilton's unfounded fear limited her activities in the classroom and robbed her of fully experiencing the joy of Christmas.

Unfounded fear can have a devastating effect on people's lives, by controlling their thoughts and actions to the point of emotional paralysis. What's more, it can result in a host of chronic physical problems like headaches, insomnia, and overwhelming fatigue.

As a teacher in the twenty-first century, you have any number of valid fears, given the threat of school violence, the instability of some of your students, and the potential for litigation being brought against you. Valid fears, the kind that are grounded in reality, send out strong signals that danger is imminent, giving you an opportunity to get out of harm's way. You *know* a threat is real.

To combat either kind of fear, prayer is the most immediate and powerful antidote you can use. When you call on God to intervene in the situation, He will allay your fears and surround you with His comforting presence. If you are in the habit of memorizing Scripture, pray a verse or two back to God, in your own words: "God, You're there to help me, and I'm not going to be afraid. What can anyone really do to hurt me, anyway? You will take care of me no matter what" (based on Hebrews 13:6). His Word will provide the peace you need.

Don't allow fear to rule your life; let God rule your life instead. Give your fears to God. Acknowledge His Lordship over all of life—and over danger, both real and imagined.

I Will

Give my fears to God. _yes_ _no_

Recognize the harmful effects of unfounded fear. _yes_ _no_

Allow God's comforting presence to surround me when I am afraid. _yes_ _no_

Be thankful for warning signals—often involving a physical reaction, like a racing heartbeat—when real danger is imminent. _yes_ _no_

Develop the habit of praying Scripture, such as Psalm 27, back to God. _yes_ _no_

Pray for God's protection over my students. _yes_ _no_

Stop letting fear rob me of my joy. _yes_ _no_

Things to Do

☐ *Write down your fears and give the list to God.*

☐ *Prepare a lesson on ways to handle fear, to use when the need arises— for example, a tragedy that impacts the school or a national crisis.*

☐ *Memorize Psalm 23 or another appropriate section of Scripture to recite when you feel afraid.*

☐ *Pray several Scriptures about God's protection back to Him in your classroom tomorrow, before the students arrive.*

☐ *Browse through the Christian Living section in a bookstore and find a book to read on fear that suits your needs.*

☐ *The next time you are afraid, begin writing—your thoughts, a poem, a prayer, whatever helps you express your deepest feelings.*

Things to Remember

David said: "The LORD, who delivered me from the paw of the lion and from the paw of the bear, He will deliver me from the hand of the Philistine." And Saul said to David, "Go, and the LORD be with you!"

1 SAMUEL 17:37 NKJV

When [Saul] came to Jerusalem, he tried to join the disciples, but they were all afraid of him, not believing that he really was a disciple.

ACTS 9:26 NIV

The Lord said to Ezekiel: "I'll make your face as hard as rock, harder than granite. Don't let them intimidate you. Don't be afraid of them, even though they're a bunch of rebels."

EZEKIEL 3:9 THE MESSAGE

David wrote: "Even if I walk through a very dark valley, I will not be afraid, because you are with me. Your rod and your walking stick comfort me."

PSALM 23:4 NCV

Then on that same first day of the week, when it was evening, though the disciples were behind closed doors for fear of the Jews, Jesus came and stood among them and said, Peace to you!

JOHN 20:19 AMP

> To the pure in heart nothing really bad can happen. Not death but sin should be our great fear.
>
> —A. W. TOZER

> Fear not; the things you are afraid of are quite likely to happen to you, but they are nothing to be afraid of.
>
> —JOHN MACMURRAY

Respect

Good Conduct

Have reverence for Christ in your hearts, and honor him as Lord. Be ready at all times to answer anyone who asks you to explain the hope you have in you, but do it with gentleness and respect.
—1 PETER 3:15–16 GNT

If you live in one of the states that has passed, or is considering, a school courtesy law, you are aware of the premise of the legislation: When students are required to speak respectfully to their teachers—using titles like *Mr.*, *Mrs.*, and *Ms.*, and responding to questions using *Sir* and *Ma'am*—courteous behavior is likely to follow. Advocates of the laws, which are generally aimed at elementary schoolchildren, see the measure as a first step toward inspiring politeness and acceptable behavior in school and society.

Respect, though, must always find a home on a two-way street. It does little good to require students to speak respectfully if the faculty members do not treat their colleagues or the students in a courteous way. The same goes for the way you discuss those in authority, such as government officials. Your manner of speaking reflects your attitude toward and opinion of others, just as it reflects on your relationship with God and the impact He has had on your life.

Respect was seemingly in short supply in the world Jesus knew, with cultures and religious groups clashing with some regularity and each group belittling the other with caustic mockery. The call by the writers of the New Testament to believers to treat everyone with gentleness, love, and respect was a radical departure from the behavior of much of the society around them. That call remains alive and well today, in a society in which it's difficult to even come to a consensus on the basic principles of common courtesy.

You are in an ideal position to live out the New Testament call to respect and model it for your students. The way you speak to and treat your students is crucial. When a student's unruly behavior tempts you to make some not-so-polite remark, consider how you would respond if that same child were a guest in your home. A simple shift in thinking such as that can immediately prompt you to react in a more respectful way. Remember the importance of your body language, too. Polite words delivered with a disapproving facial expression quickly lose their power and their intended effect.

Modeling respect for your students is an important step toward engendering respectful attitudes and behaviors in their lives. But it's much more than that: It's "the gospel in plain clothes," to paraphrase Frankie Byrne's quotation. Showing respect for others is a way of saying "Yes, Sir" to God, one that springs not from legislation but from a condition of the heart.

I Will

Treat my students respectfully. _yes_ _no_

Refer to colleagues and those in authority in a courteous manner. _yes_ _no_

Realize that my students may not understand "common courtesy" to mean the same things that I do. _yes_ _no_

Be aware that my actions reflect my attitudes. _yes_ _no_

Show reverence for God in the way I react toward others. _yes_ _no_

Remember that my body language needs to convey respect. _yes_ _no_

Things to Do

☐ Create a grade- or subject-appropriate game, research project, or role-playing scenario designed to show students the effect of respectful behavior on others.

☐ Use "Sir" and "Miss" in talking to your students tomorrow, and be prepared for a lively discussion on respect.

☐ List the names of as many people in authority over you as you can think of—from your immediate supervisor to the U.S. president—and add them to your prayer list.

☐ Watch the movie Pay It Forward, making note of how small acts of respect can pay huge dividends.

☐ Discuss school courtesy standards with other teachers to determine if new behavioral guidelines are needed in your school. Be willing to follow up.

Things to Remember

All slaves who believe must give complete respect to their own masters. In this way no one will speak evil of God's name and what we teach.

1 TIMOTHY 6:1 GOD'S WORD

Be responsive to your pastoral leaders. Listen to their counsel. They are alert to the condition of your lives and work under the strict supervision of God. Contribute to the joy of their leadership, not its drudgery. Why would you want to make things harder for them?

HEBREWS 13:17 THE MESSAGE

Kings will be like fathers to you; queens will be like mothers. They will bow low before you and honor you; they will humbly show their respect for you. Then you will know that I am the Lord; no one who waits for my help will be disappointed.

ISAIAH 49:23 GNT

The centurion said to Jesus: "I also am a man under authority, having soldiers under me. And I say to this one, 'Go,' and he goes; and to another, 'Come,' and he comes; and to my servant, 'Do this,' and he does it."

MATTHEW 8:9 NKJV

When I approach a child, he inspires in me two sentiments: tenderness for what he is, and respect for what he may become.

—LOUIS PASTEUR

Respect is love in plain clothes.

—FRANKIE BYRNE

Trust in God

Healthy Dependence

David wrote: "Our heart shall rejoice in Him, because we have trusted in His holy name."

—PSALM 33:21 NKJV

Miss McDonnell looked out at the sea of eager young faces and took a deep breath. What was she thinking when she accepted this job? After taking a heavy load each semester in college and graduating a full semester early, she had looked forward to a nice long break between her graduation in December and the start of the next school year, when she was to begin teaching third grade.

But then the school district that hired her called in January; the current third-grade teacher had been forced to retire prematurely due to physical problems. Would Miss McDonnell be available to step in early? Of course, she had said, a bit disappointed that her travel plans had to be put on hold but excited about actually stepping into the classroom, meeting the children, and getting on with her career.

But now, she was not so sure she had made the right decision. Had she acted rashly? She had prayed about it and believed she had followed God's leading in saying yes. Furthermore, her parents were in complete agreement, and the chaplain at her college—who had been her counselor and spiritual mentor for the past year—also gave his blessing. Still, she couldn't help feeling overwhelmed and very much out of her league.

Maybe you can relate to the way Miss McDonnell felt that very first day in a classroom. Most teachers say they experienced feelings of uncertainty and inadequacy on day one—and for some time to follow. Many questioned their decision to go into teaching altogether.

In those times—and at all other times, as a matter of fact—you can find the peace you need by learning to trust God completely, believing that He will do what is best for you and depending on Him to see you through those rough patches everyone experiences. He is trustworthy, faithful, and true to His Word. He loves you and wants you to have what the Bible calls an "abundant life"—a life overflowing with all that is good.

Maybe you did not have the foresight to commit your plans to God in advance, as Miss McDonnell did, or maybe you came to have faith in Him after you made a series of decisions that you now question, like the choice of your career or your mate. Even so, you can call Him to guide you and give you the wisdom and grace to handle the situation you are in. No matter what your relationship with God has been like in the past, you can always approach Him without fear or hesitation.

One of the keys to trusting God is believing that He knows your needs, your hopes, and your desires better than you do—and accepting His will even when it conflicts with what you would like to see happen. It's on this point that some people begin to falter in their ability to trust God. But they have confused trusting Him to do what's best with expecting Him to do *their* will. By their actions, they demonstrate that they have more faith in themselves than in God.

Each time you accept God's will, even when it conflicts with your own, your faith in Him deepens, especially when you see the results of doing things His way. You disagree with the heavy-handed way the principal deals with behavior problems and try to transfer to another school in the district, but your application is denied. You decide to place the situation in God's hands—and the *principal* ends up being transferred. Or a godly friend challenges him and his methods gradually change. Or, best scenario of all, he notices how effectively and graciously *you* handle behavior problems, and he begins to follow your example.

It's pointless to try to guess how God will work in the thorny situations in your life; it's much better to let it happen and be constantly amazed at His creative means of problem solving. You will know that you are truly trusting Him when you are able to let go completely, believing He will direct you in the way you should go.

I Will

Realize that God can be trusted to do what is best for me.

yes _____   *no* _____

Understand that things often happen for reasons I may not be able to see.

yes _____   *no* _____

Believe that God will see me through the rough spots in my life.

yes _____   *no* _____

Begin to start living the abundant life God wants me to have.

yes _____   *no* _____

Be aware that questioning a decision doesn't mean it was a wrong decision.

yes _____   *no* _____

Things to Do

☐ *Buy a motivational poster about trust for your classroom (even without Scripture—if yours is a public school—it can serve as a reminder for you).*

☐ *Write in your journal about a time when you experienced a blessing by trusting God.*

☐ *Read Luke 11:1–13, in which Jesus illustrates the extent to which you can trust God.*

☐ *Spend five to ten minutes meditating on trusting God.*

☐ *List any reasons you may have for not trusting a particular person, then ask God to repair the relationship and re-establish trust.*

☐ *Pray the Lord's Prayer, found in Matthew 6:9–13, focusing on your dependence on God.*

Things to Remember

Happy are those who have the God of Jacob to help them and who depend on the LORD their God, the Creator of heaven, earth, and sea, and all that is in them. He always keeps his promises.

PSALM 146:5–6 GNT

You don't even know what your life tomorrow will be! You are like a puff of smoke, which appears for a moment and then disappears. What you should say is this: "If the Lord is willing, we will live and do this or that."

JAMES 4:14–15 GNT

Depend on the Lord and his strength;
always go to him for help.
Psalm 105:4 NCV

It is dangerous to be concerned with what others think of you, but if you trust the Lord, you are safe.

PROVERBS 29:25 GNT

He keeps his eye on all who live honestly, and pays special attention to his loyally committed ones.

PROVERBS 2:8 THE MESSAGE

Pay attention to what you are taught, and you will be successful; trust in the LORD and you will be happy.

PROVERBS 16:20 GNT

Trust in the LORD with all your heart, and lean not on your own understanding. In all your ways acknowledge Him, and He shall direct your paths.

PROVERBS 3:5–6 NKJV

The psalmist wrote: "So shall I have an answer for him who reproaches me, for I trust in Your word."

PSALM 119:42 NKJV

Many sorrows shall be to the wicked; but he who trusts in the LORD, mercy shall surround him.

PSALM 32:10 NKJV

David wrote: "Some people trust the power of chariots or horses, but we trust you, LORD God."

PSALM 20:7 CEV

Suddenly David was in even worse trouble. There was talk among the men, bitter over the loss of their families, of stoning him. David strengthened himself with trust in his GOD.

1 SAMUEL 30:6 THE MESSAGE

The Scripture says, "Whoever believes on Him will not be put to shame."

ROMANS 10:11 NKJV

The very vastness of the work raises one's thoughts to God, as the only one by whom it can be done. This is the solid comfort—he knows.

—FLORENCE NIGHTINGALE

There is no other way of living piously or justly than that of depending on God.

—JOHN CALVIN

Fairness

Teacher's Pet

Jesus said: "Just as you want men to do to you, you also do to them likewise."

—Luke 6:31 NKJV

When it comes to fairness, teachers often appear to be in a no-win situation. No matter how impartially you believe you treat your students, someone is likely to accuse you of favoritism, unfairness, or, in the upper grades, injustice. It's just not fair, is it?

Inequity often exists only in the eyes of the beholder, but for you as a teacher, those eyes are important. Forget for a moment those students who equate fairness with always getting their own way. Instead, take seriously the concerns of the student who thinks you show favoritism by granting privileges more often to the girls rather than boys, or to the A students rather than the C students, or to another teacher's child over just about anyone else in the class.

You would be wise to address the situation as soon as it comes to your attention whether those concerns have any basis in reality or not. With older students, that should be no problem—some are quick to blurt out

"That's not fair!" even as you're speaking. With younger or shyer students, you may have to rely on other factors—overheard remarks, body language (like rolled eyes or even blinked-back tears), or the ever-present school grapevine.

How you deal with perceived unfairness depends in large part on the age of the student. You need to approach high-school students on an adult level, despite their pre-adult status. Drawing a student aside who has labeled you as unfair and asking, "What do you think I need to do to correct this?" can do wonders for a teenager's self-esteem—and perception of you. With very young students, the best route may be to begin tracking how often you call on certain students or students of a certain gender.

Fairness, of course, involves more than favoritism. The amount of homework you give, a "trick" question on a test, a pop quiz, revoking privileges because of misbehavior, giving a student detention—all these things are likely to be labeled as unfair, no matter how legitimate they are. Your responsibility, though, is to continue to do your job in a professional manner, with compassion and grace and mercy but professionally nonetheless.

God has a great deal to say about justice, impartiality, equity, and fairness; the Bible addresses those topics so frequently that you can readily see how important they are to Him. Ask Him to show you how to treat your students fairly and respond graciously to those who accuse you unjustly. If anyone can create a win-win scenario for you and your students, it's God.

I Will

Treat my students fairly. _____ yes _____ no

Understand how important justice is to God. _____ yes _____ no

Grant privileges to my students on an equal basis. _____ yes _____ no

Respond in a professional manner at all times. _____ yes _____ no

Address charges of unfairness immediately and tactfully. _____ yes _____ no

Believe God can turn a no-win stalemate into a win-win victory. _____ yes _____ no

Be sensitive to students who are unable to voice their feelings about being overlooked. _____ yes _____ no

Things to Do

☐ *Create an appropriate and gracious stock response to use whenever a student says, "That's not fair!"*

☐ *Keep a tally and compare how often you call on girls and on boys; you'll probably start alternating automatically to avoid having to keep track.*

☐ *Give serious thought to what it means to be a professional and write down areas for improvement.*

☐ *Look up words relating to justice in a concordance and begin reading the corresponding verses.*

☐ *Recall the things you considered unfair as a student. If, as a teacher, you still consider them to be unfair, resolve to never do those things to your students.*

Things to Remember

"I have set a time for judgment," says God, "and I will judge with fairness."

PSALM 75:2 GNT

Let them sing before the LORD, because he is coming to judge the world. He will judge the world fairly; he will judge the peoples with fairness.

PSALM 98:9 NCV

God said: "Do you know what I want? I want justice—oceans of it. I want fairness—rivers of it. That's what I want. That's all I want."

AMOS 5:24 THE MESSAGE

His ever expanding, peaceful government will never end. He will rule forever with fairness and justice from the throne of his ancestor David. The passionate commitment of the LORD Almighty will guarantee this!

ISAIAH 9:7 NLT

These are the things you should do: Tell each other the truth. In the courts judge with truth and complete fairness.

ZECHARIAH 8:16 NCV

God has set a day that he will judge all the world with fairness, by the man he chose long ago. And God has proved this to everyone by raising that man [Jesus] from the dead!

ACTS 17:31 NCV

Fair play is primarily not blaming others for anything that is wrong with us.

—ERIC HOFFER

We all have weaknesses. But I have figured out that others have put up with mine so tolerantly that I would be less than fair not to make a reasonable discount for theirs.

—WILLIAM ALLEN WHITE

Competitiveness

Peer Review

Be kindly affectionate to one another with brotherly love, in honor giving preference to one another.

—Romans 12:10 NKJV

For the past six years, the drama department at Washington High School had grown significantly. What started out as a single elective class had blossomed into a program full of passionate students eager to express themselves in ways that had never before been available. The credit was due to Mr. Rodriguez, the drama teacher who had spent almost every waking hour inventing new ways to have his students come to class excited and ready to participate.

Soon, the school needed another drama teacher, and Mr. Holt was hired to assist Mr. Rodriguez with the expansion of the program. Although the two men generally had the same goals, the change in the department brought other changes as well. Mr. Holt, a recent graduate, wanted to prove himself to the students and other teachers, while Mr. Rodriguez feared any erosion of his authority would reverse the progress the department had made. The teachers began competing for the admiration of the students.

Soon enough, the atmosphere in the department began to deteriorate, as did the quality of group rehearsals and performances. The following semester, enrollment in the drama classes decreased for the first time since its start. Mr. Rodriguez decided to take the initiative to talk things over with his colleague.

The two men shared the reasons for their insecurity and agreed to compare their methods and goals. Mr. Rodriguez sat in on a few of Mr. Holt's classes and shared several tips he had learned through years of experience. In turn, Mr. Holt observed Mr. Rodriguez's classes and offered some fresh ideas for teaching drama that had been introduced at the college he attended. They stopped competing and began working together for the good of the students and the department. The students' performances began to improve.

The pressure to succeed is enormous for teachers. Not only must you make the grade and do your job well, but you also have a deep desire to see your students leave your class better students—and better people—than they were when they arrived. When a fellow teacher appears to be doing a better job than you are, it is natural for you to step up to the challenge and become the best version of yourself that you can be. That's a good standard of measure to remember: Compete with yourself only. Cooperate with your colleagues. Strive to work together for the greater good. Allow your individual strengths and weaknesses to complement each other.

I Will

Take time to examine how my colleagues and I
can benefit from each other's strengths.

yes   _no_

Get to know my coworkers on a more personal
level.

yes   _no_

Pray for the ability to put away my competitiveness
and learn from others.

yes   _no_

Find ways to achieve my personal goals without
hindering the performance of others.

yes   _no_

Make sure that I am working for the common
good.

yes   _no_

Compete only with myself.

yes   _no_

Things to Do

☐ _List three areas of weakness in your teaching. Create a concrete plan to improve in those areas._

☐ _Sit down with a teacher you have felt competitive toward and simply have a friendly conversation._

☐ _Look up at least five verses in the Bible about teamwork or group effort. Brainstorm as to how you can apply those verses to your situation at school._

☐ _Begin an "idea" file based on what you have learned by observing your colleagues._

☐ _Compliment a competitive coworker on a job he or she has done particularly well._

Things to Remember

If anyone competes in athletics, he is not crowned unless he competes according to the rules.

2 TIMOTHY 2:5 NKJV

If you have raced against others on foot, and they have tired you out, how can you compete with horses? If you stumble in open country, how can you live in the jungle along the Jordan River?

JEREMIAH 12:5 GOD'S WORD

Jesus said: "That they may all be one, as You, Father, are in Me, and I in You; that they also may be one in Us, that the world may believe that You sent Me."

JOHN 17:21 NKJV

Do you not know that in a race the runners all compete, but only one receives the prize? Run in such a way that you may win it.

1 CORINTHIANS 9:24 NRSV

Jesus said: "You're blessed when you can show people how to cooperate instead of compete or fight. That's when you discover who you really are, and your place in God's family."

MATTHEW 5:9 THE MESSAGE

The only person you should ever compete with is yourself. You can't hope for a fairer match.

—TODD RUTHMAN

Do your work with your whole heart, and you will succeed—there's so little competition.

—ELBERT HUBBARD

Conflict

Divine Intervention

Repay no one evil for evil. Have regard for good things in the sight of all men. If it is possible, as much as it depends on you, live peaceably with all men.

—ROMANS 12:17–18 NKJV

Megan tugs at the stuffed giraffe Tim is playing with as Tim clutches it close to him with all his might. Jason and his friends run Stephen and *his* friends off the neighborhood basketball court with verbal assaults about their geekiness. Dana's not talking to Tiesha and is making life miserable for their mutual friends. All this spills over to affect the dynamics in their respective classrooms, where their teachers are doing their best to avoid being distracted by tense, ongoing contract negotiations that may result in a district-wide faculty walkout.

The potential for conflict in the classroom and on the campus is ever-present. From subtle psychological pressure to schoolyard bullying to out-and-out violence, young people have any number of tactics at their disposal to incite disagreement and stir up a fight. And adults—well, their years and experience have provided them with even more ways of provoking conflict.

With all of this anger and dissension simmering below the surface—and even erupting on occasion—you may wonder what you are doing in that kind of environment. You may even begin to think that it can't possibly be God's will for you to stay there. After all, the Bible speaks so often about the Christian life being a life filled with peace. Yet on some days you experience a whole lot more conflict than peace.

What God promises, however, is inner peace, not absence of conflict. No matter where you work, what your career, or what your circumstances, conflict will always be a possibility. Your response to it is what makes the difference in how it affects you. Let it get to you, and you will lose your peace. Use it as a springboard to become a peacemaker, and you will grow in your faith. It really is up to you.

The ideal situation is to prevent contention before it begins. In the classroom, that requires an extra measure of vigilance on your part. Mocking, teasing, name-calling, gossip, spreading rumors—at every age and every grade level—all contribute to tension among students. You're the one in authority and in control, and it's your responsibility to let your students know that you will not tolerate those kinds of things in your classroom. Be prepared to follow up.

The same is true for jealousy between individuals and rivalry between groups. At the first indication of trouble, you need to intervene according to the policies your school has established. You also have a means of intervention that supersedes school policy and exerts far more influence and power on the parties involved in any kind of conflict: prayer. When you first notice that trouble is brewing, that's a good time to go to God and talk the situation over with Him, asking

Him to intervene and show you how you can help stop the conflict before it ever gets started.

If a dispute does erupt into a fight, always remember that the safety of your students must be your primary concern, and you need to rely on the immediate guidance God gives you to determine the best course of action for you to take. That's one of the reasons why maintaining a close relationship with God is so important—in the heat of a crisis, you can trust the direction He gives, because you have the assurance of knowing that it *is* His direction and not your own thoughts. You've learned to identify His "voice"—that inner sense of guidance that His Spirit gives—because you've listened to His voice in quieter and more peaceful times.

You may feel like a referee at times, but as a believer, your role in resolving conflict is that of a mediator and a peace-maker. When a conflict arises that is in your jurisdiction to handle, ask God to give you wisdom and allow you to see the larger picture—focusing not on who is right or who is more right or who started it, but on the underlying principle involved in the dispute.

A world filled with strife was not God's plan for His creation. But with His help, you can work toward preventing conflict, resolving disputes, and keeping the peace in your own world. You may not always be as successful at it as you would like, but you can be confident that God is with you in the midst of conflict.

I Will

Make every effort to prevent disputes before they begin.

yes   no
_____   _____

Strive to be a mediator and peacemaker to resolve conflict.

yes   no
_____   _____

Understand that the potential for conflict exists in every job.

yes   no
_____   _____

Cultivate hearing God's voice before a crisis hits.

yes   no
_____   _____

Make the safety of my students my primary concern.

yes   no
_____   _____

Ask God for wisdom to see the larger issues involved in a dispute.

yes   no
_____   _____

Things to Do

☐ *Make sure you are familiar with your district's current policies for handling violence in the classroom.*

☐ *Read Romans 12:17–18 and Proverbs 26:20 in several translations (available online) and memorize the verses in a translation that appeals to you.*

☐ *Clearly post a ban on inflammatory language and behavior in your classroom.*

☐ *Enlist the help of colleagues in creating an age-appropriate object lesson on conflict to keep on hand to use the next time a dispute arises in your classroom.*

☐ *Remind your students of the consequences of stirring up trouble.*

☐ *Think back to a time in your life when conflict resulted in emotional growth or a deeper trust in God, and write about it in your journal.*

Things to Remember

Paul wrote: "Good-by, my friends. Do better and pay attention to what I have said. Try to get along and live peacefully with each other. Now I pray that God, who gives love and peace, will be with you."

2 CORINTHIANS 13:11 CEV

The beginning of strife is like releasing water; therefore stop contention before a quarrel starts.

PROVERBS 17:14 NKJV

By pride comes nothing but strife, but with the well-advised is wisdom.
Proverbs 13:10 NKJV

Shun youthful lusts and flee from them, and aim at and pursue righteousness (all that is virtuous and good, right living, conformity to the will of God in thought, word, and deed); [and aim at and pursue] faith, love, [and] peace (harmony and concord with others) in fellowship with all [Christians], who call upon the Lord out of a pure heart.

2 TIMOTHY 2:22 AMP

Paul wrote: "My goal is that they will be encouraged and knit together by strong ties of love. I want them to have full confidence because they have complete understanding of God's secret plan, which is Christ himself."

COLOSSIANS 2:2 NLT

If you keep attacking each other like wild animals, you had better watch out or you will destroy yourselves.

GALATIANS 5:15 CEV

Better to dwell in a corner of a house-top, than in a house shared with a contentious woman.

PROVERBS 21:9 NKJV

Now, the effects of the corrupt nature are obvious: illicit sex, perversion, promiscuity, idolatry, drug use, hatred, rivalry, jealousy, angry outbursts, selfish ambition, conflict, factions.

GALATIANS 5:19–20 GOD'S WORD

[A conceited person] shows that he doesn't understand anything. Rather, he has an unhealthy desire to argue and quarrel about words. This produces jealousy, rivalry, cursing, suspicion, and conflict between people whose corrupt minds have been robbed of the truth. They think that a godly life is a way to make a profit.

1 TIMOTHY 6:4–5 GOD'S WORD

Avoid foolish disputes, genealogies, contentions, and strivings about the law; for they are unprofitable and useless.

TITUS 3:9 NKJV

Whenever you're in conflict with someone, there is one factor that can make the difference between damaging your relationship and deepening it. That factor is attitude.

—TIMOTHY BENTLEY

Difficulties are meant to rouse, not discourage. The human spirit is to grow strong by conflict.

—WILLIAM ELLERY CHANNING

Honesty

Always True

He who would love life and see good days, let him refrain his tongue from evil, and his lips from speaking deceit.

—1 PETER 3:10 NKJV

Everyone in the community seemed to know Mrs. Rothman. In her seventeen years of faithful service at the town's high school, she had an established reputation as an excellent teacher, but there was something else about her that earned the admiration of those around her: the swarm of students that seemed to surround her at all times. It was not surprising to walk into her classroom at any time of day to find her tutoring, counseling, or simply sharing stories with a student. Young people trusted and respected her on a level unfamiliar to many of her peers.

One day a newcomer to the profession asked why her students responded to her in such a positive way. Somewhat taken aback, Mrs. Rothman could only repeat an observation made by a previous student. "Every year, on the first day of school, I have a tradition," she said. "Before I mention books or homework, I tell the students a little bit about myself. More specifically, I tell them what kind of a teacher I am—what I'm good at, what I'm not so good at. I tell them I am continually learning just as they are."

That, her former student said, was what helped her establish a great relationship with her students.

Mrs. Rothman's students also knew that she would always answer their questions to the best of her ability and would always come clean when she didn't know the answer to one of their questions. "I simply teach them what I know and understand. If a question or situation arises and I don't know the answer, I love to say, 'I don't know—but let's figure it out together,'" she said. Her honesty and openness created a comfortable, natural environment in which she was able to interact with the students. "The things you can achieve when you are open with your students are far more rewarding than I had thought possible," she added.

One virtue that people seem to universally respect is honesty, even among people who are not necessarily honest themselves. Being completely truthful is a challenging standard to set for your classroom and for yourself, but it's a standard that allows for transparent communication between you and your students. You have no need to play the part of the flawless, omniscient teacher, and your students are less likely to try to put one over on you. Your honesty and openness will provide a relaxed learning atmosphere—and earn for you a healthy measure of respect.

I Will

Hold myself accountable for my words and actions.　　_yes_　　_no_

Ask God to help me to be more honest in my everyday challenges.　　_yes_　　_no_

Decide that I will not only speak honestly but also live honestly.　　_yes_　　_no_

Realize that being truthful goes a long way toward building trust and respect.　　_yes_　　_no_

Immediately begin to pray whenever I face the temptation to lie.　　_yes_　　_no_

Admit to God and others when I have been anything less than honest.　　_yes_　　_no_

Things to Do

☐ Create a suggestion box for your students to comment on the classroom atmosphere and your teaching methods.

☐ Admit that you don't know the answer the next time you are confronted with a question that stumps you and enlist your students' help in finding the answer.

☐ Schedule one-on-one sessions with students in order to be able to communicate freely about work progress without classroom politics interfering.

☐ Confess your dishonesty and ask the forgiveness of someone you've been untruthful with recently.

☐ Encourage your students to be truthful by reminding them that a legitimate reason beats a dishonest excuse every time.

Things to Remember

Paul said: "Believe me, I do my level best to keep a clear conscience before God and my neighbors in everything I do."

ACTS 24:16 THE MESSAGE

Paul wrote: "In the presence of Christ, I speak with utter truthfulness—I do not lie—and my conscience and the Holy Spirit confirm that what I am saying is true."

ROMANS 9:1 NLT

The mouth of the righteous brings forth wisdom, but the perverse tongue will be cut out.

PROVERBS 10:31 NKJV

Dishonest scales are an abomination to the LORD, but a just weight is His delight.

PROVERBS 11:1 NKJV

He who speaks truth declares righteousness, but a false witness, deceit.

PROVERBS 12:17 NKJV

A false witness shall perish, but the man who hears him will speak endlessly.

PROVERBS 21:28 NKJV

The commandment of absolute truthfulness is really only another name for the fullness of discipleship.

—DIETRICH BONHOEFFER

May those whose holy task is to guide impulsive youth, fail not to cherish in their souls a reverence for truth.

—CHARLOTTE FORTEN GRIMKE

Goals

Multiple Choice

Paul wrote: "One thing I do, forgetting those things which are behind and reaching forward to those things which are ahead, I press toward the goal for the prize of the upward call of God in Christ Jesus."

—PHILIPPIANS 3:13–14 NKJV

You already know what it takes to meet a goal in your life. You wanted to be a teacher, and you accomplished that goal. Now, with myriad responsibilities and challenges vying for your attention, you may have this nagging awareness in the back of your mind that you should continue to set goals for your life, but there never seems to be enough time to give goal-setting the attention it deserves.

If that's the case, start small. Jot down things you'd like to do, whenever the thought occurs to you; a small, palm-sized voice recorder is great for something like this. Don't restrict yourself to professional goals. Maybe you want to learn to fly or do an in-depth study of the book of Revelation. Write down and record everything.

When you have a few minutes, pick just one item on your list. Say you've always wanted to go back to school and earn a master's in education, but you don't want to relocate and uproot your children, and you don't know how your family would survive without your income anyway. Take that one item and do just one activity related to that goal. For example, do some online research. You may discover that the very school you wish to attend now offers a distance learning program that would allow you to earn most of your credits online, and that the site has links to numerous organizations that offer grants to teachers who want to continue their education.

If you keep taking incremental steps like that toward each of your goals, you'll be on your way toward earning your pilot's license and mastering the book of Revelation in no time. Sometimes the enormity of an accomplishment is all it takes to discourage people from pursuing their passions in life. But once you get in the habit of turning each desire into an achievable goal and breaking that goal into smaller steps, your aspirations shrink to manageable proportions.

So go ahead—dream big. Invite God into the process and ask Him to help you refine your goals and bring them into line with His will. Pray about them every step of the way. Keep track of your progress; little by little you'll realize that you are actually getting closer to the goal line. Once you reach a goal, remember to celebrate. And while you're at it, remember to thank God and anyone else who helped you along the way.

I Will

Ask God to help me set achievable goals for my life.

yes _____ no _____

Break larger goals down into smaller steps to avoid frustration.

yes _____ no _____

Express my gratitude to everyone who helped me achieve my aspirations.

yes _____ no _____

Celebrate each time I meet a goal in my life.

yes _____ no _____

Dream big.

yes _____ no _____

Appreciate all that I've already accomplished.

yes _____ no _____

Refuse to become discouraged when my goals seem unattainable.

yes _____ no _____

Things to Do

☐ Start a list of goals for your life—personal, spiritual, and professional.

☐ Read Philippians 3:7–21, in which Paul describes his aspirations and encourages believers to have similar goals.

☐ Look over the next big project you'll be assigning, and make sure you break it down into smaller steps for your students.

☐ Choose a goal you've had in mind for a long time and consider the reasons why you haven't achieved it—and how that's going to change.

☐ Set aside some time this week—even if it's only fifteen minutes or so—to work on just one of your goals.

☐ Seek the prayer support of several people as you strive to meet one of your more difficult goals.

Things to Remember

Paul wrote: "Everyone who competes for the prize is temperate in all things. Now they do it to obtain a perishable crown, but we for an imperishable crown."

1 Corinthians 9:25 nkjv

Looking unto Jesus, the author and finisher of our faith, who for the joy that was set before Him endured the cross, despising the shame, and has sat down at the right hand of the throne of God.

Hebrews 12:2 nkjv

As long, then, as that promise of resting in him pulls us on to God's goal for us, we need to be careful that we're not disqualified.

Hebrews 4:1 the message

Paul wrote: "I have not yet reached my goal, and I am not perfect. But Christ has taken hold of me. So I keep on running and struggling to take hold of the prize."

Philippians 3:12 cev

The vision will still happen at the appointed time. It hurries toward its goal. It won't be a lie. If it's delayed, wait for it. It will certainly happen. It won't be late.

Habakkuk 2:3 god's word

No one can be making much of his life who has not a very definite conception of what he is living for.
—Washington Irving

It's kind of fun to do the impossible.
—Walt Disney

Motivating Others

Infectious Inspiration

Nehemiah wrote: "Then I told them about how the gracious hand of God had been on me, and about my conversation with the king. They replied at once, 'Good! Let's rebuild the wall!' So they began the good work."

—NEHEMIAH 2:18 NLT

The "motivational" industry has seen explosive growth in the past decade. People whose names were once unknown now attract celebrities, statesmen, and even former presidents to speak at their one-day motivational events that attract tens of thousands of people at each venue on the speakers' cross-country tours. Add to that the motivational workshops and seminars aimed specifically at teachers, and you have an abundance of events to choose from if you ever feel you need a fresh shot of inspiration to jump-start your motivational battery.

That wasn't Mr. Polk's problem—he had been a highly motivated teacher ever since the first day he set foot in the high school where he had been teaching for the past fifteen years. The problem, as he saw it, was the students' motivation. Many of them seemed to lack very much motivation at all unless they were vying for a top honor or admission to a highly competitive college. His wife, who taught fifth grade, reported a similar problem, with motivation at that grade level tied closely to grades and comments on report cards. Dismayed at the lack of enthusiasm for learning itself, the couple decided to explore the reasons why children lacked motivation.

Their research uncovered a host of explanations for the problem—little parental support, social ills, the school funding crisis, and the like. The solutions seemed out of their control They couldn't force parents to get involved any more than they could correct society's problems or produce more money for education.

During dinner one night with several friends who were also teachers, Mrs. Polk expressed her frustration and mentioned the data they had uncovered. "The best thing you can do is to examine yourself. You might still feel just as motivated as you always have, but are you inspiring your students as much as you always did?" asked one of Mr. Polk's colleagues in the history department who had heard students commenting on his less-than-inspiring presentations.

That started a lively discussion about how to challenge students by enabling them to see education and learning as tools they could use to paint a picture of their future or weave the tapestry of their lives or fashion a sculpture that would give form to their hopes and expectations. The metaphors were hardly in short supply as each teacher created an image of what inspiration looks like in the lives of young people.

An inspiring lesson, message, or piece of writing prompts people of all ages to dream—and dream big. As the teachers sat around the table that night, they talked about the elements that factor in to inspiring others to dream big: A vision for the future. Pure delight in people—in their case, children—just as they are. A nonjudgmental, safe environment in which questioning and curiosity and even failure can exist without fear of ridicule. Warmth and sensitivity. A loving and caring attitude. Being awakened to a potential that is based in reality and not insincere praise.

That night, the Polks realized that although they were both good teachers, they had come close to giving up emotionally on the students they cared so much about. As a result, they hadn't been particularly inspirational of late. They stayed up well into the night, sharing ideas and helping each other think of new and creative ways they could motivate their students. The change in their classrooms didn't come overnight, but the change in their thinking did.

The story in the Bible of Nehemiah shows how one person can inspire a group of people to accomplish a task that others have not even thought possible. Nehemiah refused to give up, asked God to have favor on him, and soon had others sharing in his vision. Though he would face many obstacles, and the work itself would be long and hard, he continued to keep the people in his charge motivated and on the job.

Help your students get on track with realizing their potential by creating a learning environment that inspires them to think beyond their present circumstances. Give them a vision for their future that transcends the everydayness of their school experience and offers them a reason to believe that what they're learning today will benefit them tomorrow.

I Will

Periodically examine my effectiveness in motivating my students.

yes _____ *no* _____

Seek to inspire rather than simply teach just to convey information.

yes _____ *no* _____

Create a safe learning environment that is free of ridicule.

yes _____ *no* _____

Strive to show each student his or her potential.

yes _____ *no* _____

Give my students hope for the future.

yes _____ *no* _____

Ask God to have favor on me in my efforts to be a motivator of youth.

yes _____ *no* _____

Things to Do

☐ *Place a tape or CD on motivating others in your car to listen to on the way to and from school and on longer trips.*

☐ *Read how Nehemiah inspired the people to rebuild the walls of Jerusalem in chapters one and two of the book of Nehemiah.*

☐ *Look over your lesson plan book to see how much variety you've used in your teaching techniques, and plan your next week's lessons with more variety.*

☐ *Schedule calls to the parents or guardians of your students—not to discuss problems but to encourage them and let them know you care.*

☐ *Create a "success plan" for your students, showing them how a step-by-step strategy can help them accomplish their bigger dreams.*

☐ *Select an upcoming lesson and transform it into an interactive, hands-on activity that will appeal to less-motivated students.*

Things to Remember

The heart of the wise teaches his mouth, and adds learning
to his lips.

PROVERBS 16:23 NKJV

Jesus said: "David himself, speaking under the inspiration of the
Holy Spirit, said, 'The LORD said to my Lord, Sit in honor at my
right hand until I humble your enemies beneath your feet.' "

MARK 12:36 NLT

*A bad motive can't achieve a good end;
double-talk brings you double trouble.*
Proverbs 17:20 THE MESSAGE

The spirit of a man is the lamp of the LORD, searching all the
inner depths of his heart.

PROVERBS 20:27 NKJV

Would not God search this out? For He knows the secrets
of the heart.

PSALM 44:21 NKJV

David said: "My son Solomon, acknowledge the God of your
father, and serve him with wholehearted devotion and with a
willing mind, for the LORD searches every heart and understands
every motive behind the thoughts. If you seek him, he will be
found by you; but if you forsake him, he will reject you forever."

1 CHRONICLES 28:9 NIV

Those who live at the ends of the earth stand in awe of your wonders. From where the sun rises to where it sets, you inspire shouts of joy.

PSALM 65:8 NLT

Paul wrote: "We can understand someone dying for a person worth dying for, and we can understand how someone good and noble could inspire us to selfless sacrifice."

ROMANS 5:7 THE MESSAGE

Paul wrote: "It is for this we labor and strive, because we have fixed our hope on the living God, who is the Savior of all men, especially of believers."

1 TIMOTHY 4:10 NASB

Jesus responded, "Then why does David, speaking under the inspiration of the Holy Spirit, call him Lord? For David said, 'The LORD said to my Lord, Sit in honor at my right hand until I humble your enemies beneath your feet.'"

MATTHEW 22:43–44 NLT

Charge Joshua and encourage him and strengthen him, for he shall go across at the head of this people, and he will give them as an inheritance the land which you will see.

DEUTERONOMY 3:28 NASB

The mediocre teacher tells. The good teacher explains. The superior teacher demonstrates. The great teacher inspires.

—WILLIAM W. WARD

A teacher who is attempting to teach without inspiring the pupil with a desire to learn is hammering on a cold iron.

—HORACE MANN

Contentment

Satisfaction Guaranteed

Paul wrote: "Not that I speak in regard to need, for I have learned in whatever state I am, to be content."
—Philippians 4:11 NKJV

It's Saturday night, and you're looking over your lesson plans for the coming week to make sure you have everything you need. Even as you think that thought, another one occurs to you: *Everything I need. Wouldn't that be great, just once?* Already this month you've spent more of your own money on classroom supplies than your budget can safely handle. Your students have to share their outdated textbooks, the teacher's edition was so marked up by previous years' teachers that you can barely make sense of it, and there's talk of slashing your school's meager budget even more next year. On Friday, after making a dozen transparencies for Monday's lesson, you discovered that two of the school's three overhead projectors are on the fritz and the third is nowhere to be found.

Mix all that together, and you have a perfect recipe for teacher discontent. The main ingredient is there: less than enough of everything, it seems, for the students, the teachers, and the school. At times you wonder how anyone can expect teachers to do their job at an optimum level when the tools they need are provided at a minimal level. But somehow, you always manage, making do and being creative despite the deep frustration you feel.

Contentment is often an elusive quality. It's especially hard to achieve when you *know* that what you need is attainable. A wealthier school district can afford to buy new textbooks for each student—and teacher—and enough equipment to go around. It's all beyond your grasp and out of your hands.

Finding contentment may seem like a difficult endeavor, but all it takes is a change in attitude. When you shift your focus to what you have instead of what you don't have (or what *they* have), you discover that you already possess a great deal to work with and a great deal to be thankful for. You learn to rely on your own ingenuity and resourcefulness to compensate for the lack of tangible tools available to you.

Of course, when you have God in your life, you can find fulfillment and satisfaction in knowing that He has provided and will continue to provide for your needs. That provision may not always look the way you would like it to, especially when it comes to the quantity of the provision, but you can be assured that God knows what He's doing. He has provided everything you need—over and over again.

I Will

Learn to be content. _____ yes _____ no

Realize that God is the One who provides what
I need. _____ yes _____ no

Be thankful for what I have. _____ yes _____ no

Learn to creatively compensate for what I don't
have. _____ yes _____ no

Share with other teachers those resources that
I do have. _____ yes _____ no

Understand that God's way of meeting my needs
may not be what I had in mind. _____ yes _____ no

Things to Do

☐ *Think of the one item you wish you had most for your classroom.
Come up with three creative alternatives to that item.*

☐ *Walk around your classroom and genuinely thank God for all the
inadequate, patched-together, and outdated equipment and supplies
you have to work with.*

☐ *Memorize Philippians 4:11–12 and resolve to apply its truth to
your life.*

☐ *Browse through a bookstore or library to find a suitable—and
affordable—book on contentment or simplified living.*

☐ *Go online and read several stories about mission workers, such as
George Mueller, who learned to depend on God for their daily
provision—literally.*

Things to Remember

There is one who makes himself rich, yet has nothing; and one who makes himself poor, yet has great riches.

PROVERBS 13:7 NKJV

David wrote: "Bless the LORD, O my soul, and forget not all His benefits."

PSALM 103:2 NKJV

The psalmist wrote: "You, LORD, have made me glad through Your work; I will triumph in the works of Your hands."

PSALM 92:4 NKJV

Mary said: "He has satisfied the hungry with good things and sent the rich away with empty hands."

LUKE 1:53 NLT

Paul wrote: "I know what it is to be in need, and I know what it is to have plenty. I have learned the secret of being content in any and every situation, whether well fed or hungry, whether living in plenty or in want."

PHILIPPIANS 4:12 NIV

It's better to obey the LORD and have only a little, than to be very rich and terribly confused.

PROVERBS 15:16 CEV

Contentment is a pearl of great price, and whoever procures it at the expense of ten thousand desires makes a wise and happy choice.

—JOHN BALGUY

A little is as much as a lot, if it is enough.

—STEVE BROWN

Time Management

After Hours

Walk circumspectly, not as fools but as wise, redeeming the time, because the days are evil.

—EPHESIANS 5:15–16 NKJV

Mrs. Geller's job as a middle-school English instructor required more work than she could possibly expect to get done on the clock. She had a full—no, an overflowing—plate. Waking up before dawn, she filled her day with tutoring, thinking of ways to keep her classes interesting, grading tests and homework, and attempting to find a few moments of peace in between the rush of adolescent children entering and exiting her room.

After school, Mrs. Geller had to pick up her own children from daycare, get any necessary shopping done, attempt to prepare a nutritious dinner, tidy up the house, and spend time with her family. That usually left about fifteen good minutes to finish grading papers before she collapsed into bed.

Like many teachers, Mrs. Geller rarely finished the things she set out to do in a single day. She knew her students viewed her as an "easy" teacher; it was difficult to expect her students to adhere to deadlines when she couldn't. Plus, she felt she was missing out on precious time with her own children. But with her full workload, she had no time to work out a solution.

Then, one January morning, school was canceled due to a snowstorm. In her typical "must get everything done" frame of mind, she used the time to catch up on grading papers, planning next week's lessons, and doing the laundry. To her surprise, by midafternoon she had nothing urgent left to do. She invited a snow-shoveling neighbor in for a hot cup of coffee and spent a treasured, quiet evening with her family.

At the end of her surprise vacation day, Mrs. Geller realized what a burden her busy schedule had become. In her frenzy to get everything done—a feat no one ever accomplishes—she had been working against time rather than with it. The following Saturday morning, she sat down with her husband and worked out a schedule for managing the daily work of running a household. That afternoon, she spent three uninterrupted hours brainstorming about ways she could streamline her work-related tasks and manage her workload more efficiently.

The Bible tells you not to worry about tomorrow, but sometimes it is difficult to keep that in mind when life demands that you do twenty-four hours worth of tasks in eighteen hours. But few people benefit from a frantic schedule. On the contrary, most people suffer, along with everyone around them. Bring God into your schedule planning; He invented time, and He can help you manage it. When you come up with a reasonable schedule—and stick to it as much as possible—the pressure eases up, and you are far more likely to accomplish what you set out to do.

I Will

Work *with* time instead of *against* it.

yes   no

Take the time to come up with solutions to my
time management problems.

yes   no

Realize that no one ever gets everything done;
there will always be something else to do.

yes   no

Ask God to help me create a realistic schedule
for my personal and professional life.

yes   no

Guard against the habit of racing through life
at a frantic pace.

yes   no

Take full advantage of God-sent breaks and
blessings, like an unexpected day off.

yes   no

Things to Do

☐ *Use your computer to save time by creating templates of frequently used forms and documents.*

☐ *Go through your lesson plan book and schedule time for planning, paperwork, and work-related reading (including professional development materials).*

☐ *Search online for sites that offer lesson plans that you can use when you're pressed for time.*

☐ *Ask for parents' e-mail addresses and create a group listing in your address book for sending notices home. Print out messages for students without e-mail.*

☐ *Call a family meeting to create a manageable schedule for chores and relaxation.*

Things to Remember

Remember now Your Creator in the days of your youth, before the difficult days come, and the years draw near when you say, "I have no pleasure in them."

ECCLESIASTES 12:1 NKJV

To everything there is a season, a time for every purpose under heaven.

ECCLESIASTES 3:1 NKJV

He who keeps his command will experience nothing harmful; and a wise man's heart discerns both time and judgment.

ECCLESIASTES 8:5 NKJV

A thousand years in Your sight are like yesterday when it is past, and like a watch in the night.

PSALM 90:4 NKJV

Mordecai said to Esther: "If you remain silent at this time, relief and deliverance will arise for the Jews from another place and you and your father's house will perish. And who knows whether you have not attained royalty for such a time as this?"

ESTHER 4:14 NASB

God says, "At just the right time, I heard you. On the day of salvation, I helped you." Indeed, God is ready to help you right now. Today is the day of salvation.

2 CORINTHIANS 6:2 NLT

How you spend your time is more important than how you spend your money. Money mistakes can be corrected, but time is gone forever.

—DAVID B. NORRIS

Half our life is spent trying to find something to do with the time we have rushed through life trying to save.

—WILL ROGERS

Silent Witness

[Jesus] said to them, "Go into all the world and preach the gospel to every creature."

—MARK 16:15 NKJV

Karen couldn't imagine a better life than the one she had. A history teacher in a Christian high school, Karen had come to love her work—and the assistant pastor of the church that sponsored the school. David returned the favor, and they married six months to the day after their first date.

Within a year, David was called to a senior pastorate in a rural community in Nebraska. The Johnsons wanted to pay off their student loans quickly, and to do that, Karen needed to work. But the only Christian schools in the vicinity of their new hometown were K–8, and none was hiring. That left one possibility: teaching at a regional public high school that just happened to need a history teacher.

Karen took the job, but her hopes of cultivating close relationships with other Christian teachers, and building solid spiritual principles into the lives of her students, seemed to evaporate before her eyes. The regional school was so much larger than she was accustomed to. The 1 to 15 teacher to student ratio she once enjoyed was a thing of the past; now she had thirty-plus students in every class, and trying to accomplish *anything*—from getting through a lesson to getting a message to the guidance office—was far more complicated.

Worst of all, Karen no longer felt as useful to God as she had at her former school. She was used to openly talking about God and Jesus and the Bible, and she began leaving campus each afternoon feeling increasingly discouraged. She was so distracted by her concerns about school that she kept up a running conversation with God about the situation for an entire weekend—even during her beloved husband's sermon that Sunday morning.

On Monday, during her first free period, Amanda, a quiet student in her second period American history class, came to her classroom and asked if they could talk. It took a while for Amanda to get past the awkwardness, but finally she said, "I don't know if I'm even allowed to ask you this, but . . . are you a Christian?" Somewhat taken aback, Mrs. Johnson confirmed she was a believer and that they could talk about her faith since Amanda had initiated the conversation.

Relieved, Amanda slowly opened up about problems at home that were interfering with her schoolwork. Just before the bell rang, Mrs. Johnson quietly prayed for her. As she got up to leave, Amanda thanked her, explaining that she and her friends figured Mrs. Johnson just had to be a Christian, because she was always so kind to everyone. Over the following weeks, students began to trickle in during Mrs. Johnson's free period, knowing that there they could find a listening ear and a kind heart.

Like Karen, you may not have any inkling of the impact you are making on your students through your silent witness for God. But your unspoken influence on them could have far-reaching and life-changing consequences. God's Spirit has a way of revealing Himself, and His activity in your life, simply through who you are. Most of the time you won't have a clue what it was that tipped people off; in fact, most of the time they won't know either.

Anglican cleric Lindsay Dewar believes each Christian stands as either a wall or a bridge between people and God. Your very demeanor can help build a portion of a bridge without your having to say a word about God. For Amanda and her friends, it was Mrs. Johnson's kindness that revealed God's activity in her life. For someone else, it may be her servanthood or her joy or any number of other godly qualities that show her to be a Christian.

Remember, too, that even if you work in a public school, you don't need to remain silent about God if a student is the first to bring up the subject of faith. Karen discovered that she *could* talk about God in school, as long as she waited for Him to prompt someone else to initiate the conversation. The incident with Amanda taught Karen a valuable lesson—in her own classroom. When you trust God completely to use you as a positive influence in your students' lives, His Spirit is free to work through the person to whom you are to reveal the God He is.

I Will

Be a positive influence—and a positive example of
a Christian—in the lives of others.
yes _____ _no_ _____

Demonstrate my faith in God in the way I live
my life.
yes _____ _no_ _____

Ask God to help me publicly acknowledge my
faith when appropriate.
yes _____ _no_ _____

Learn how to legally share my faith with my
students and colleagues.
yes _____ _no_ _____

Realize that my actions reveal the extent of my
trust in God.
yes _____ _no_ _____

Things to Do

☐ *Read Acts 17:22–31 to gain insight into Paul's skill at discussing faith in a non-Christian environment.*

☐ *Familiarize yourself with your First Amendment rights in the classroom by reading related articles prepared by the American Center for Law and Justice (www.aclj.org).*

☐ *Schedule a lunch or break with Christian colleagues to discuss how you can appropriately demonstrate your faith in the classroom.*

☐ *Create a lesson on religion—complete with Bible passages—that complies with your district's guidelines.*

☐ *Prepare a standard response—one that clarifies the legal boundaries— to give if a student ever initiates a conversation about faith.*

☐ *Subscribe to an e-newsletter, such as one of several from the Family Research Council (www.frc.org), to stay informed about First Amendment issues in the classroom.*

Things to Remember

Jesus said, "When the Holy Spirit has come upon you, you will receive power to testify about me with great effect, to the people in Jerusalem, throughout Judea, in Samaria, and to the ends of the earth, about my death and resurrection."

ACTS 1:8 TLB

Daily in the temple, and in every house, they [believers] did not cease teaching and preaching Jesus as the Christ.

ACTS 5:42 NKJV

Jesus said, "You are the light of the world. A city that is set on a hill cannot be hidden."
Matthew 5:14 NKJV

Paul wrote: "To me, who am less than the least of all the saints, this grace was given, that I should preach among the Gentiles the unsearchable riches of Christ."

EPHESIANS 3:8 NKJV

Paul wrote: "I make known to you, brethren, that the gospel which was preached by me is not according to man. For I neither received it from man, nor was I taught it, but it came through the revelation of Jesus Christ."

GALATIANS 1:11–12 NKJV

Jesus said, "No one can come to Me unless the Father who sent Me draws him; and I will raise him up at the last day."

JOHN 6:44 NKJV

Jesus said: "The Good News about the Kingdom will be preached throughout the whole world, so that all nations will hear it."

MATTHEW 24:14 NLT

Jesus said: "Go therefore and make disciples of all the nations, baptizing them in the name of the Father and of the Son and of the Holy Spirit."

MATTHEW 28:19 NKJV

Jesus said: "As you go, announce that the kingdom of heaven will soon be here."

MATTHEW 10:7 CEV

Jesus said: "But before the end comes, the good news must be preached to all nations."

MARK 13:10 CEV

Jesus said: "Whatever I say to you in the dark, you must tell in the light. And you must announce from the housetops whatever I have whispered to you."

MATTHEW 10:27 CEV

Preach God's message. Do it willingly, even if it isn't the popular thing to do. You must correct people and point out their sins. But also cheer them up, and when you instruct them, always be patient.

2 TIMOTHY 4:2 CEV

> Every life is a profession of faith, and exercises an inevitable and silent influence.
>
> —HENRI FREDERIC AMIEL

> Every one comes between men's souls and God, either as a brick wall or as a bridge. Either you are leading men to God or you are driving them away.
>
> —CANON LINDSAY DEWAR

Vigilance

Eyes in the Back of Your Head

Be sober, be vigilant; because your adversary the devil walks about like a roaring lion, seeking whom he may devour.

—1 Peter 5:8 NKJV

The news on the front page of Tuesday's paper sickened the community: A student had assaulted a young girl in the back of an eighth-grade classroom—while the teacher continued the math lesson, apparently oblivious to the traumatic, and criminal, activity. In addition to leveling understandable outrage at the abuser, people expressed horror and disbelief that such a thing could take place in school, in a supervised classroom.

What the paper did not report was that the student had planned the incident well. A friend of the attacker had purposely created a potentially dangerous distraction in the front of the room, drawing Mr. Colbert's attention from the back of the room. Although the truth eventually came out—with one student after another challenging the accuracy of the newspaper account and testifying on behalf of the teacher—the public outcry was so great that it forced Mr. Colbert to uproot his family and leave the district entirely to seek a teaching position where no one knew him.

There's no question that teachers need to maintain constant vigilance throughout the school day. You've probably experienced incidents in your own classroom that made you wish you had eyes in the back of your head, as well as surveillance cameras all around the room. Wishing hasn't made that happen, however, and some days it's just impossible to see and hear everything that goes on around you. God's Spirit, who is everywhere, does see and hear everything. By developing a sensitivity to His warning signs, you can be one step ahead when a dangerous situation arises.

Sometimes, He will alert you to danger by redirecting your attention—or revealing to you a person's inner motives, such as those of the accomplice who created the distraction in Mr. Colbert's class. He may prompt a student to tell you about a rumored threat against the student body, or He may simply give you a sense deep within that something is terribly wrong. He will also give you the ability to see and hear far more than seems humanly possible, especially when danger is nearby.

Danger comes in many forms, including a threat to your spiritual life. Just as you need to be vigilant on campus, you also need to be watchful when it comes to the wily schemes of your ultimate adversary, who would destroy your relationship with God in a heartbeat if he could. Knowing he can't, he tries to pick away at it little by little. But God's Spirit is on to his ways, and He will alert you when Satan is getting dangerously close. Guard your spiritual life the way you guard your classroom, with continual vigilance—and reliance on God's Spirit.

I Will

Be aware of my immediate surroundings at
all times.

yes   _no_

Keep the safety of my students in the forefront
of my mind.

yes   _no_

Realize that the potential for danger is
always present.

yes   _no_

Learn to face danger with an unwavering trust
in God.

yes   _no_

Guard my spiritual life.

yes   _no_

Respond immediately when I sense God's Spirit
sending me a warning sign.

yes   _no_

Things to Do

☐ Thoroughly examine your school district's policies and procedures for handling harmful situations.

☐ Read what Jesus said about the need for constant vigilance in Mark 13:35–40.

☐ Mentally rehearse a typical day in your classroom, noting situations when your routine may make you less vigilant.

☐ Make your class aware of your "zero tolerance" policy when it comes to threats to the students' safety—before anyone has a chance to test your limits.

☐ Brainstorm with a group of teachers about ways to minimize the potential for danger without creating an aura of fear in your classrooms.

Things to Remember

The end of all things is at hand; therefore be serious and watchful in your prayers.

1 PETER 4:7 NKJV

Be watchful in all things, endure afflictions, do the work of an evangelist, fulfill your ministry.

2 TIMOTHY 4:5 NKJV

Jesus said, "If he comes suddenly, do not let him find you sleeping. What I say to you, I say to everyone: 'Watch!'"

MARK 13:36–37 NIV

Jesus said, "Watch and pray, lest you enter into temptation. The spirit indeed is willing, but the flesh is weak."

MARK 14:38 NKJV

Continue in prayer, and watch in the same with thanksgiving.

COLOSSIANS 4:2 KJV

Therefore let us not sleep, as do others; but let us watch and be sober.

1 THESSALONIANS 5:6 KJV

Beware of rashness, but with energy, and sleepless vigilance, go forward and give us victories.

—ABRAHAM LINCOLN

No man is entitled to the blessings of freedom unless he be vigilant in its preservation.

—DOUGLAS MACARTHUR

Trustworthiness

Keeping Your Word

Paul wrote: "You have heard me teach many things that have been confirmed by many reliable witnesses. Teach these great truths to trustworthy people who are able to pass them on to others."

—2 TIMOTHY 2:2 NLT

Whenever the time came each year to select a senior class adviser at Harding High School, the entire faculty knew who would be selected for the responsibility. Gretchen Rausch had held that position for years, and for good reason. Sure, she was a popular teacher, and the students gravitated toward her because of her cheerful disposition and willingness to listen to them. But there was more to Mrs. Rausch than that—much more.

Early in her career, Mrs. Rausch had witnessed the aftermath of two incidents at the first school where she worked. First, the junior-senior prom, which promised to be the best ever in the history of that school, had to be canceled, all because the faculty adviser had failed to keep his word. He claimed that he had booked an elaborate banquet hall at a discounted rate, but the school discovered—one week before the event—that he hadn't cleared his under-the-table deal with the hall's owners, and a wedding had dibs on the hall that night. In the second incident, someone in the guidance department had leaked confidential information about a student. The leak devastated the student and her family and prompting a lawsuit against the district.

To be sure, mistakes happen, but in both of those cases, the actions taken were willful and deliberate. Students and parents found it difficult to trust any teacher or administrator they did not know well, and the school's efforts to smooth things over through a series of town meetings did little to restore their trust. Mrs. Rausch saw firsthand what happens when trust in the school system is seriously eroded. In her personal life as well as her professional life, she adhered to a number of trust-producing principles, including maintaining confidences, always telling the truth, and adhering to the axiom to under-promise and over-deliver.

Mrs. Rausch wisely knew that she needed to rely on God to adhere to those principles. Because she did that, she consistently acted in a way that earned her the trust of the students, their parents, and her colleagues. That meant more responsibility was placed on her, but she thoroughly enjoyed working with the seniors and guiding them through their journey toward postgraduation life. Today she maintains that the trust she worked so hard to build up has been richly rewarded, over and over again, with the joy that came from taking on that extra responsibility.

I Will

Believe that God is trustworthy.

Keep my word.

Prove myself trustworthy to those I have disappointed in the past.

Show that I can be trusted to keep confidential information to myself.

Expect greater responsibility as a result of others' trust in me.

Under-promise and over-deliver.

Understand that it may take time for some people to realize they can trust me.

Things to Do

☐ *Choose someone in the Bible who was considered trustworthy—Isaac's son Joseph, for example, or Daniel—and read about his or her life.*

☐ *Identify trustworthy people in your subject area and discuss in class what set these people apart—for example, a highly respected politician for civics class or a journalist for English class.*

☐ *Think about Henry Lewis Stimson's quote on the facing page in light of your own life; list the people whose trust in you helped you to become more trustworthy, and thank God for those people.*

☐ *Ask yourself, "Why in the world would anyone trust me?" Write down as many answers as you can think of.*

☐ *Write a brief article on the importance of trustworthiness as a character trait for teachers and submit it to a publisher of a teachers' magazine, journal, or devotional.*

Things to Remember

Jesus said: "I have so many things to say that concern you, judgments to make that affect you, but if you don't accept the trustworthiness of the One who commanded my words and acts, none of it matters. That is who you are questioning—not me but the One who sent me."

JOHN 8:26 THE MESSAGE

The other supervisors and governors tried to find reasons to accuse Daniel about his work in the government. But they could not find anything wrong with him or any reason to accuse him, because he was trustworthy and not lazy or dishonest.

DANIEL 6:4 NCV

Jesus said: "He said, 'Good servant! Great work! Because you've been trustworthy in this small job, I'm making you governor of ten towns.' "

LUKE 19:17 THE MESSAGE

No one who gossips can be trusted with a secret, but you can put confidence in someone who is trustworthy.

PROVERBS 11:13 GNT

Managers are required to be trustworthy.

1 CORINTHIANS 4:2 GOD'S WORD

The only way to make a man trustworthy is to trust him.

—HENRY LEWIS STIMSON

Men of genius are admired, men of wealth are envied, men of power are feared; but only men of character are trusted.

—SOURCE UNKNOWN

Role Modeling

Front and Center

Paul wrote: "Imitate me, just as I also imitate Christ."

—1 Corinthians 11:1 NKJV

As a teacher, you stand front and center every day when you are in the classroom—and even when you are not. Whether you realize it or not, you are someone's role model, and almost certainly, a role model for several students. You can't help that. There's nothing you can do to change the fact that on a daily basis, someone out there is taking in all that you do and say and storing it away for future emulation.

That can be a daunting thought. But it wasn't for the apostle Paul, at least not later in his life when he wrote his magnificent letters to the Corinthian church. That's because Paul was himself a good student. He so imitated the life of his master, Jesus, that he had no problem suggesting that others imitate him. If that sounds arrogant, consider this possibility: Paul loved Jesus so much that he lived his life in such a way that his behavior would never bring dishonor to Jesus' name. That's not arrogance; that's honor. Paul honored his Master—and the best role model a person could ever have—by living an exemplary life.

That's good news for you, because if Paul, "the chief of all sinners," can successfully imitate Christ, then there's hope that you can too. To do that, though, you need to know Jesus and examine those qualities that have made Him worthy of emulation for the past two thousand years. Keep that in mind whenever you read the Gospel accounts of His life. In the meantime, take a look at some of the qualities that permeated His life and drew so many people to follow Him.

First, even though He was God Himself, He trusted His Father in heaven to lead Him during His thirty-plus years on earth. Even at Gethsemane on the night before His crucifixion, knowing full well that His mission was about to be fulfilled, He turned to the Father and sought His strength and His comfort and His assurance that what was about to come to pass was indeed the Father's will.

Second, He not only loved, He *was* love. The Bible says "God is love" (1 John 4:8). Since Jesus is God, He also is love itself. Jesus revealed His love for the Father and for people in every single thing He did, even when He overturned the moneychangers' tables and drove out of the temple area the merchants who sold livestock and doves. His love for the Father would not allow for anything that dishonored Him; His love for the people is recounted in so many stories, both written and unwritten, that "the world itself would not contain the books that would be written" (John 21:25 NASB).

Third, Jesus valued everyone. People know when they're valued, and that holds just as true for your students as it does for those who followed Jesus in first-century Palestine. You know that every single child in your care, no matter how promising, how exasperating, how bright, how difficult, any individual child is, every one is valuable in the eyes of God. You can imitate Jesus by letting your students know the value you place on their lives each time you give them your undivided attention and a listening ear and even the occasional benefit of the doubt.

Fourth, Jesus spent much of His ministry years teaching others, and teaching them creatively. He took advantage of every teaching opportunity to open the eyes of His followers to the truth in often new and startling ways. He was a master storyteller and a skilled communicator, and even a sometime humorist. People came from miles around, presumably at considerable sacrifice, to listen to Him, and it was always worth whatever sacrifice they made.

Jesus had many more qualities worth imitating, but if you could master just those four, you'd be an exceptional role model indeed. If your love for Jesus is like Paul's, you're already living a life that seeks to honor Him. By consciously emulating Jesus, you too may one day be able to say to others, "Imitate me, just as I imitate Christ."

I Will

Make Jesus my role model.

yes   *no*

Remember that as a teacher, I am automatically a role model.

yes   *no*

Realize that even outside the classroom, my students are watching.

yes   *no*

Be thankful that I have God's Spirit to help me live an exemplary life.

yes   *no*

Trust God to make me a good role model for my colleagues and the parents of my students.

yes   *no*

Relax and be myself.

yes   *no*

Things to Do

- [ ] *Read Philippians 3:17 and determine if, like Paul, you could honestly say to someone, "Pattern your life after mine."*

- [ ] *John Milton said the goal of education is to know, love, and imitate God. Determine how you can fulfill the goal of leading your students to make Jesus their role model.*

- [ ] *Identify one of the main problems in your classroom (tardiness, lack of preparation) and think of ways you can model the opposite trait.*

- [ ] *List the qualities that you consider essential for a good role model to have; rate yourself against the list you just created.*

- [ ] *Meditate on Ephesians 5:1 and what it means to imitate God.*

- [ ] *Ask your students who their role models are and why. Lead them in a discussion about the need to choose role models of good character.*

Things to Remember

Let no one despise your youth, but be an example to the
believers in word, in conduct, in love, in spirit, in faith, in purity.

1 TIMOTHY 4:12 NKJV

Therefore take up the whole armor of God, that you may be able
to withstand in the evil day, and having done all, to stand.

EPHESIANS 6:13 NKJV

*David wrote: "My life is an example to
many, because you have been my
strength and protection."*
Psalm 71:7 NLT

Paul wrote: "Dear brothers, pattern your lives after mine and
notice who else lives up to my example."

PHILIPPIANS 3:17 TLB

Your word is a lamp to my feet and a light to my path.

PSALM 119:105 NKJV

In everything set them an example by doing what is good.

TITUS 2:7 NIV

Be imitators of God as dear children.

EPHESIANS 5:1 NKJV

You received the message with joy from the Holy Spirit in spite of the severe suffering it brought you. In this way, you imitated both us and the Lord. As a result, you yourselves became an example to all the Christians in Greece.

1 THESSALONIANS 1:6–7 NLT

He did what was pleasing in the LORD's sight and followed the example of his ancestor David. He did not turn aside from doing what was right.

2 KINGS 22:2 NLT

Jesus said: "I have given you an example to follow. Do as I have done to you."

JOHN 13:15 NLT

Paul wrote: "And now, dear brothers and sisters, we give you this command with the authority of our Lord Jesus Christ: Stay away from any Christian who lives in idleness and doesn't follow the tradition of hard work we gave you. For you know that you ought to follow our example. We were never lazy when we were with you."

2 THESSALONIANS 3:6–7 NLT

"Our father is Abraham," they declared. "No," Jesus replied, "for if you were children of Abraham, you would follow his good example."

JOHN 8:39 NLT

If doing good in public will excite others to do more good, then . . . "Let your Light shine to all . . ." Miss no opportunity to do good.

—JOHN WOSLEY

The greatest power for good is the power of example.

—AUTHOR UNKNOWN

Sacrifice

On the Altar

Paul wrote: "I beseech you therefore, brethren, by the mercies of God, that you present your bodies a living sacrifice, holy, acceptable to God, which is your reasonable service."

—ROMANS 12:1 NKJV

Every teacher knows the names and the stories: Shannon Wright, who died while shielding a student from shooters at a Jonesboro, Arkansas, middle school in 1998; Dave Sanders, who was killed while trying to lead students to safety in the Columbine rampage—teachers who have made the ultimate sacrifice for their students. Many others have survived shootings and other forms of violence as they protected the lives of those entrusted to their care.

Theirs are the sacrificial acts that make the headlines, and rightfully so. Still, every day teachers make sacrifices, both big and small, on behalf of their students. To those educators, teaching is much more than a job. It's a calling and a responsibility that is to be cherished, because the future of the children in their care is at stake.

Many teachers have made significant sacrifices to become, and remain, teachers; with their education, they could no doubt land a much cushier job at a higher salary, but still, they choose to stay because their students need them, or they believe in the value of education, or they know this is God's will for their lives. Whatever the reason, they've sacrificed a measure of comfort for a higher purpose. Many teachers make daily sacrifices for their students—time spent tutoring instead of taking a break or leaving for the day; money out of their own pockets to make sure this one has paper and pencils or that one eats lunch today.

Think about the things you've given to, or given up for, your students. Did you consider those to be sacrifices? Probably not—people tend to think big when they hear the word *sacrifice*. *The American Heritage Dictionary of the English Language* defines an act of sacrifice as the "forfeiture of something highly valued for the sake of one considered to have a greater value or claim." That's nicely put, especially in light of the amount of time—something highly valued—that you give up for your students, those who are considered to have a greater value.

Never diminish the significance of the sacrifices you make in the course of your school day. God doesn't. He knows how important a contribution you are making toward the lives of the students you teach and interact with each day. He places a high value on your sacrificial acts, even those that will never make front-page news.

I Will

Thank God for sending His Son to sacrifice His life for me.

yes _____ _no_ _____

Find opportunities for little, daily sacrificial acts on behalf of others.

yes _____ _no_ _____

Appreciate sacrifice as a privilege, not an obligation.

yes _____ _no_ _____

Have a joyful attitude toward giving up something to please God.

yes _____ _no_ _____

Realize that in order to emulate Jesus, I must sacrifice my selfish desires.

yes _____ _no_ _____

Learn to loosen my grip on the things I love and may have to sacrifice one day.

yes _____ _no_ _____

Things to Do

☐ _Watch, or mentally recall, the crucifixion scenes portrayed in Mel Gibson's film_ The Passion of the Christ _and meditate on Jesus' sacrifice for you._

☐ _Spend focused time in prayer asking God to show you what He would like you to give up; write down what you sense His answer is and commit yourself to making the resulting sacrifice._

☐ _Read the story of Abraham and Isaac on Mount Moriah (Genesis 22:1–18) in light of your own willingness to sacrifice something you love._

☐ _Like the "good shepherd" in John 10, teachers sometimes put themselves in harm's way to protect their students; let such a colleague know how much you appreciated his or her sacrificial act._

☐ _1 Samuel 15:22 indicates that to the Lord, obedience is better than sacrifice. Reflect on the ways that applies to your experience with God._

Things to Remember

This is love: not that we loved God, but that he loved us and sent his Son as an atoning sacrifice for our sins.

1 JOHN 4:10 NIV

Walk in love, as Christ also has loved us and given Himself for us, an offering and a sacrifice to God for a sweet-smelling aroma.

EPHESIANS 5:2 NKJV

Don't forget to do good things for others and to share what you have with them. These are the kinds of sacrifices that please God.

HEBREWS 13:16 GOD'S WORD

Jesus said, "God so loved the world that He gave His only begotten Son, that whoever believes in Him should not perish but have everlasting life."

JOHN 3:16 NKJV

We love Him because He first loved us.

1 JOHN 4:19 NKJV

May my prayer be set before you like incense; may the lifting up of my hands be like the evening sacrifice.

PSALM 141:2 NIV

If Jesus Christ be God and died for me, then no sacrifice can be too great for me to make for Him.

—C. T. STUDD

Let others laugh when you sacrifice desire to duty, if they will. You have time and eternity to rejoice in.

—THEODORE PARKER

Determination

Relentless Pursuit

As for us, we have this large crowd of witnesses around us. So then, let us rid ourselves of everything that gets in the way, and of the sin which holds on to us so tightly, and let us run with determination the race that lies before us.

—HEBREWS 12:1 GNT

Even as a teenager, Donna Howard was known for going after whatever she wanted with a steely resolve, whether it was the state record in track or the top position in her graduating class in high school. That same determination followed her through college, where the tougher competition only fueled her sense of determination. When she had her eyes focused on something she wanted—a trophy, an accomplishment, any kind of goal—she pursued it relentlessly until it was hers.

That quality served her well, but it also made her more than a few enemies through the years. Now she was a teacher, and she had her sights set on the departmental chair. Those who had known her longest expected her to go after that position with a vengeance, never giving up until it was hers. What they didn't know, or acknowledge, was that her recent encounter with God was much more than the fleeting religious conversion that they assumed she would eventually get over. That encounter had changed her life, and God was in the process of making quite a few changes in Donna's character, changes that would make her and everyone around her a whole lot happier.

Those changes didn't occur overnight, but they were significant enough to show her colleagues that even though she was just as determined as ever, her focus had changed. Now, she was determined to be the best teacher, and the best person, she could be, and if that meant being promoted to the departmental chair, so be it. She would not, however, continue to ride roughshod over her colleagues to make it happen.

As Donna's old life indicated, the quality of determination can be misused. But when it's used in a positive way, and brought under the control of God's Spirit, it's a quality that can help you overcome obstacles and see a project through to completion and even make you a better person than you ever thought you could be, as you resolve to replace bad habits with productive practices. Determination is a decision of your will; you decide that you *will* finish this task or establish that spiritual practice or develop those character qualities, no matter how you feel or what stands in your way.

The best thing in life that you can relentlessly pursue, of course, is God and a life that is pleasing to Him. Approach *that* with steely determination and an unwavering inner resolve, and you'll end up accomplishing far more than the earthly goals you've set for yourself.

I Will

Run the race of life with determination.

yes___ no___

Understand the distinction between determination and stubbornness.

yes___ no___

Keep my focus on God and away from those things I perceive as obstacles.

yes___ no___

Remember that determination goes hand in hand with following God's will.

yes___ no___

Encourage others to keep going when they feel like quitting.

yes___ no___

Realize that determination is a decision of my will that does not depend on my feelings.

yes___ no___

Things to Do

☐ *Read the book of Ruth and reflect on Ruth's determination to leave her homeland so she could remain with Naomi.*

☐ *Revive an old project that you once believed in and resolve to see it through to its completion.*

☐ *List classroom activities that you are determined to do this year—and decide whether your commitment to them stems from genuine determination or stubbornness.*

☐ *Select at least one spiritual practice, such as daily prayer and occasional fasting, that you have trouble building into your routine, and determine to integrate it into your life.*

☐ *Memorize Hebrews 12:1.*

Things to Remember

"Where you die, I will die, and there I will be buried. Thus may the LORD do to me, and worse, if [anything but] death parts you and me." When she saw that she was determined to go with her, she said no more to her.

RUTH 1:17–18 NASB

When the days were approaching for His ascension, He was determined to go to Jerusalem; and He sent messengers on ahead of Him, and they went and entered a village of the Samaritans to make arrangements for Him.

LUKE 9:51–52 NASB

We rebuilt the wall, which was rebuilt to about half its [original] height. The people worked with determination.

NEHEMIAH 4:6 GOD'S WORD

Look down and see from heaven, from your holy and beautiful dwelling. Where is your determination and might? Where is the longing of your heart and your compassion? Don't hold back.

ISAIAH 63:15 GOD'S WORD

You must realize that the Lord has chosen you to build his holy Temple. Now do it—and do it with determination.

1 CHRONICLES 28:10 GNT

Let us not be content to wait and see what will happen, but give us the determination to make the right things happen.

—PETER MARSHALL

Desire is the key to motivation, but it's the determination and commitment to an unrelenting pursuit of your goal—a commitment to excellence—that will enable you to attain the success you seek.

—MARIO ANDRETTI

Prayer

Hidden Powers

Jesus said, "Whatever things you ask when you pray, believe that you receive them, and you will have them."

—MARK 11:24 NKJV

When the courts began to ban spoken prayer in public schools, those who challenged the legality of school prayer claimed a decisive victory. Despite their win, the debate over school prayer—now focused on specific circumstances instead of the general issue—has continued for more than forty years, and there's little sign of it letting up. But in all their celebrating back in the 1960s, the victors overlooked at least one facet of school prayer: the immense power wielded by an individual teacher, silently praying as her students enter her classroom.

You have hidden power in your school—the power of prayer. You can pray in every classroom, office, common area, and closet, in every nook and cranny, on every square foot of your campus. You can pray for every student, every parent, every guardian, every teacher, every administrator, and every member of the support staff. No one can stop you—and no one can stop God from hearing your prayers, because He doesn't need to hear your voice to hear your prayers.

What's more, you can be highly creative in your prayers. As a teacher, you have a multitude of means for influencing others right at your disposal. Here are some suggestions for things you can pray for in addition to the obvious, the salvation and protection of everyone on your campus:

Ask God to lead your students to talk to you about Him. If a student initiates a conversation about God, you can continue the discussion. Pray that God will give you wisdom and discernment and the right words to say in each individual circumstance. One teacher who prayed this prayer enjoyed numerous conversations about faith with students who "happened" to bring up the subject privately to him.

Ask God to help you plan lessons that contain underlying spiritual principles. No matter what your subject area, there is spiritual truth inherent in it. History, literature, science, mathematics, physical education, art, and music—all embody spiritual principles. Even business and computer classes can address spiritual issues, such as ethics and moral responsibility. Pray about your lessons; God has a wealth of ideas stored up for you.

If you're an English teacher, you can pray for an opportunity to teach the Bible as literature. The courts have upheld that freedom. Ask God to direct you as you create a lesson plan to present to the administration or school board ahead of time, and ask Him particularly to give you wisdom regarding the passages that you choose to teach.

Ask God to show you how you can apply biblical principles to behavioral problems in the classroom. You may not be able to cite chapter and verse, but you can certainly paraphrase Bible verses that address behavior without mentioning the source. Any time you read the book of Proverbs, Jesus' parables, and Paul's letters, ask God to open your eyes to spiritual truth you can convey in the classroom, without crossing the line of legality.

Ask God to prepare the hearts of your students to hear spiritual truth—and pray for the ability to impart it effectively. Your skills as a communicator will never be more important than they are when you are attempting to convey biblical principles.

Remember to listen as you pray and allow God to speak to you. Prayer is more than talking to God; it's hearing Him as well. Take off your teacher hat as you pray and become a student—a disciple—once again. Learn from Him, and apply what you've learned in prayer once you put your teacher hat back on again.

No one can strip you of the power of your prayer life. Obey the laws—as far as they go. Recognize the freedom you have to pray in your heart, to your heart's content, and exercise that freedom to the fullest extent possible. The hidden power you have is not hidden to God. God hears every single cry of your heart.

I Will

Make prayer a priority in my everyday life. _____ yes _____ no

Have faith that God hears my prayers. _____ yes _____ no

Believe that prayer not only changes things but also changes me. _____ yes _____ no

Remember to listen to what God has to say to me. _____ yes _____ no

Realize that God wants to hear from me no matter how long it's been. _____ yes _____ no

Be honest and vulnerable to God every time I talk to Him. _____ yes _____ no

Things to Do

☐ *Divide the number of children you teach by seven or thirty, depending on the size of your classes, and pray for them by name each day of the week or the month.*

☐ *Begin the practice of praying the Scriptures back to God (choose an appropriate passage, such as Psalm 5:3 or Psalm 54:2, and recite it as a prayer).*

☐ *Meet with a Christian colleague to pray together for your school, the administration, and your coworkers.*

☐ *Reflect on the two quotes about prayer on page 149 and how their perspective on prayer applies to your prayer life.*

☐ *Read about prayer in Matthew 6:5–13.*

☐ *Find a prayer partner, join a prayer group, or pray online with other Christians at www.crosswalk.com/community/prayer/—or do all three.*

Things to Remember

Paul wrote: "I want the men everywhere to pray, lifting up their hands in a holy manner, without anger and arguments."

1 TIMOTHY 2:8 NCV

Cornelius was a religious man. He and all the other people who lived in his house worshiped the true God. He gave much of his money to the poor and prayed to God often.

ACTS 10:2 NCV

This is the confidence that we have in Him, that if we ask anything according to His will, He hears us.
1 John 5:14 NKJV

We can spend our time praying and serving God by preaching.

ACTS 6:4 CEV

He shall pray to God, and He will delight in him, He shall see His face with joy, for He restores to man His righteousness.

JOB 33:26 NKJV

You, beloved, building yourselves up on your most holy faith, praying in the Holy Spirit, keep yourselves in the love of God, looking for the mercy of our Lord Jesus Christ unto eternal life.

JUDE 20 NKJV

The LORD will command His
lovingkindness in the daytime; and
His song will be with me in the night,
a prayer to the God of my life.

PSALM 42:8 NASB

Jesus said, "Where two or three are
gathered in My name, I am there in the
midst of them."

MATTHEW 18:20 NKJV

Jesus said: "If you believe, you will
receive whatever you ask for in prayer."

MATTHEW 21:22 NLT

Jesus said: "When you pray, you shall
not be like the hypocrites. For they love
to pray standing in the synagogues and
on the corners of the streets, that they
may be seen by men. Assuredly, I say to
you, they have their reward."

MATTHEW 6:5 NKJV

David wrote: "Each morning you listen
to my prayer, as I bring my requests to
you and wait for your reply."

PSALM 5:3 CEV

David wrote: "O God, listen to my
prayer. Pay attention to my plea."

PSALM 54:2 NLT

**In prayer it is
better to have a
heart without
words than words
without a heart.**

—JOHN BUNYAN

**Prayer is less about
changing the world
than it is about
changing ourselves.**

—DAVID J. WOLPE

Leadership

Advanced Standing

Do not try to rule over those who have been put in your care, but be examples to the flock.

—1 PETER 5:3 GNT

When she was introduced at a large gathering last year, Crystal Lancour was welcomed with a round of applause befitting a well-known celebrity. But until that moment, Lancour was unknown to most of the people in the room. Far from being a celebrity, Lancour is an eighth-grade math teacher who had done the unthinkable: She not only agreed to have a typical class videotaped for a study on teaching math and science but also agreed to have the recording made public. Only three other teachers out of six hundred whose classes were taped gave similar permission.

It's an unspoken assumption that teachers are reluctant to have others observe their work. But Lancour and her three unnamed colleagues stepped ahead of the pack and took a leadership role. They did this not because they thought they were better teachers or had found the secret to successful teaching but because they are ordinary teachers with ordinary classrooms who believe others could learn from what they may have done right as well as what they may have done wrong. They swallowed their pride and took the lead in order to help their colleagues find better ways of teaching their subject matter.

The Crystal Lancours of the education world not only function as leaders but also as servants. That may be a difficult concept to understand at first. But when you realize that one of the characteristics of true servants is the willingness to relinquish their personal desires and preferences on behalf of others, you can see how genuine leadership—leadership that flows from the heart—goes hand in hand with servanthood. All good teachers are servant leaders to the students in the classroom; a few are also servant leaders to others in their profession.

The Bible is replete with examples of servant leaders, the most obvious being Jesus Himself. You can find no better model of servant leadership than Him. He led with strength, love, humility, compassion, empathy, vision—and sacrifice. He *gave of* Himself to those He led, and ultimately *gave Himself* for everyone.

If you want to see a transformation in your professional life, ask God to give you the heart of a servant leader. Study the leadership style of Jesus and other heroes of the Bible, like Moses and Joshua and Joseph and Daniel. Don't be surprised when you discover that you have a radically different attitude toward teaching—as well as a radically different attitude toward life.

I Will

Lead with humility and integrity.   _yes_   _no_

Continually develop my leadership skills.   _yes_   _no_

Make sure the decisions I make as a leader line
up with biblical truth.   _yes_   _no_

Learn from Jesus' example as a leader.   _yes_   _no_

Trust God to give me the confidence I need to
lead well.   _yes_   _no_

Strive to be consistent as a leader.   _yes_   _no_

Realize that genuine leadership involves the heart
as well as the mind.   _yes_   _no_

Things to Do

☐ Visit John Maxwell's leadership site at www.injoy.com and sign up for his free monthly e-newsletter, "Leadership Wired."

☐ Take the lead in a teachers' meeting or other faculty activity.

☐ Define for yourself what you think the qualities of a good leader are, and rate yourself against your own list.

☐ Learn more about the concepts of servant leadership at www.servleader.org and teachers as leaders at www.teacherleaders.org.

☐ Test your commitment to developing your leadership skills by taking charge of a project outside your comfort zone this week.

☐ Choose a leader you respect and read about him or her, analyzing the characteristics that cause you to admire that person.

Things to Remember

Let us stop just saying we love people; let us really love them, and show it by our actions.

1 JOHN 3:18 TLB

Paul wrote to Timothy: "Here is a saying you can trust. If anyone wants to be a leader in the church, he wants to do a good work for God and people."

1 TIMOTHY 3:1 NIrV

The LORD said to Joshua, "No man shall be able to stand before you all the days of your life; as I was with Moses, so I will be with you. I will not leave you nor forsake you."

JOSHUA 1:5 NKJV

Jesus said: "It shall not be so among you; but whoever desires to become great among you shall be your servant."

MARK 10:43 NKJV

Jesus said: "Let your light so shine before men, that they may see your good works and glorify your Father in heaven."

MATTHEW 5:16 NKJV

A man is known by his actions. An evil man lives an evil life; a good man lives a godly life.

PROVERBS 21:8 TLB

True leadership must be for the benefit of the followers, not the enrichment of the leaders.

—ROBERT TOWNSEND

Leadership is action, not position.

—DONALD H. MCGANNON

Rest

Time-Out

It is vain for you to rise up early, to sit up late, to eat the bread of sorrows; for so He gives His beloved sleep.

—PSALM 127:2 NKJV

Roger Gant grew up in a family that believed in keeping the Sabbath by taking Sunday off and dedicating the entire day to the Lord. His father worked five days a week for a construction company, and ran errands and did odd jobs around the house on Saturday, being sure to get all his work done before Sunday. When Roger became a teacher, his father noticed early on that he seemed to work all the time—not just teaching in the classroom but grading papers at night and on weekends, creating lessons, and researching advanced education and grant opportunities on the Internet.

"You know, son, you need to rest from all this work," his father managed to say during a rushed phone conversation one Sunday afternoon. "Do like we've always done—take Sunday off." Roger patiently responded, "Dad, you don't understand. If I don't look over my lessons on Sunday night, I'll be lost on Monday morning. There's just no time during the school day to prepare for anything. I have to do all my preparation at home."

The elder Gant thought about that for a while before he said anything more. He believed the Sabbath was a gift from God to man, not a legalistic obligation. Sure, he hadn't had the kind of responsibility Roger now had, but still . . . the gift was for everyone, even teachers. A few days later, a solution occurred to him, and he called his son again. "Look," he said, "you know it doesn't matter to God when you take your Sabbath. How about trying this, just once, and see how it works: Take a Sabbath rest from Saturday evening until Sunday evening. That way, you'll still have Sunday evening to prepare for Monday."

Roger wasn't convinced it would work—he normally needed a good chunk of Sunday afternoon as well—but he agreed to give it a try. His father's plan worked beautifully. Twenty-four hours of rest had so refreshed his body, mind, and spirit that he was able to do all the planning he needed in far less time than it normally took. He even got to bed at a reasonable hour that Sunday night. In no time, his customized Sabbath had become a regular part of his week.

Accept this wonderful gift from God, the freedom to take one day off each week. It may take a while before it becomes a routine in your life. But remember—*any* period of undistracted rest during your hectic week, even just a few hours, will help to restore your soul and refresh your spirit.

I Will

Give myself permission to take a break when I
need one.

yes _____ _no_ _____

Be thankful that God set an example by resting
on the seventh day.

yes _____ _no_ _____

Recognize a day of rest as an opportunity to
restore my body, mind, and spirit.

yes _____ _no_ _____

Get the amount of sleep I need each night.

yes _____ _no_ _____

Trust God that the demands on my time will be
met without my health suffering.

yes _____ _no_ _____

Learn to read the signals that indicate I'm
overdoing it.

yes _____ _no_ _____

Things to Do

☐ *Look into visiting a monastery or a prayer center for a week or more
during the next summer break to truly relax.*

☐ *Finish this sentence: "My favorite way to relax is_____." Now do it.*

☐ *Try keeping one day a week as a day of rest for the next month. See if
you can continue the practice past a month.*

☐ *Develop a routine that will relax you before you go to bed—dim the
lights, read Scripture, light candles, play soothing music.*

☐ *Read what Jesus taught about the Sabbath in Mark 2:23–28, especially
the last verse.*

☐ *Meditate on Matthew 11:29.*

☐ *Read Lauren Winner's short book* Mudhouse Sabbath *to discover ways
to incorporate Jewish practices into your Christian day of rest.*

Things to Remember

The LORD said, "Six days you shall do your work, and on the seventh day you shall rest, that your ox and your donkey may rest, and the son of your female servant and the stranger may be refreshed."

EXODUS 23:12 NKJV

Abraham said, "Please let a little water be brought, and wash your feet, and rest yourselves under the tree."

GENESIS 18:4 NKJV

On the seventh day God ended His work which He had done, and He rested on the seventh day from all His work which He had done.

GENESIS 2:2 NKJV

[Jesus and His disciples] departed to a deserted place in the boat by themselves.

MARK 6:32 NKJV

Jesus said: "Take my yoke upon you. Let me teach you, because I am humble and gentle, and you will find rest for your souls."

MATTHEW 11:29 NLT

David said: "Oh, that I had wings like a dove! I would fly away and be at rest."

PSALM 55:6 NKJV

The time to relax is when you don't have time for it.

—SIDNEY J. HARRIS

No rest is worth anything except the rest that is earned.

—JEAN-PAUL FRANCOEUR

Faith

Mustard-Seed Experiment

Jesus said: "I assure you, even if you had faith as small as a mustard seed you could say to this mountain, 'Move from here to there,' and it would move. Nothing would be impossible."

—MATTHEW 17:20 NLT

As Cynthia Robertson looked out over the sea of faces in her first period art class, she wondered what the future held for the twenty-three students in the room—and a hundred others who would spend time in her classroom that day. The previous night, she and the other art teachers at Mill River High School had heard the verdict: District-wide budgetary cuts were forcing the school board to trim back the art department's budget even more than they had the year before. Without the proverbial miracle, two nontenured teachers would be let go, and the department would have to make do with equipment that had seen better days a decade ago.

Mrs. Robertson understood the conventional thinking; art was one of those expendable subject areas, not like reading or math or other skills-oriented subjects. But she and her colleagues had seen the positive effect of art class on students who found it difficult to express themselves verbally and students who needed a creative release from the academic pressure they were under—and students with emotional disorders who sorted out their lives using color and design. She believed God wanted the art program to improve, not deteriorate, and all through the summer she maintained her belief that God would come through, often calling her Christian colleagues and encouraging them to keep praying.

Before the new school year began, an announcement was made that called for a celebration: A large corporation had approved a long-forgotten grant request that would cover the salaries of the two teachers, plus allow for the purchase of new equipment and replenish the supply cabinets. The art program would continue, stronger than ever. As for Mrs. Robertson, her faith had been bolstered; though she says her faith would not have diminished even if the grant request had been denied. "God would have just come through in another way," she shrugs.

Maybe your faith is not quite as strong as Mrs. Robertson's, and maybe you find it difficult to believe for something as big as the restoration of two teachers' jobs and the ability of an entire department to provide improved instruction. That's all right with God. He just wants you to take whatever measure of faith you have, turn it over to Him, and allow Him to enlarge it.

Jesus spoke to His disciples about this kind of faith when they were unable to drive a demon out of a young boy whose life had been endangered. "I can guarantee this truth," He said to them. "If your faith is the size of a mustard seed, you can say to this mountain, 'Move from here to there,' and it will move.

Nothing will be impossible for you" (Matthew 17:20 GOD'S WORD). The smallest amount of faith can achieve the seemingly impossible when that faith is rightly placed in the God who routinely does the impossible.

Another section of the Bible, Hebrews 11, recounts what some of the great heroes of the faith discovered when they put their faith and trust in God. They had faith—the assurance of things hoped for and the evidence of things unseen—and they watched as God did exactly what He said He would do on their behalf.

Cynthia Robertson looked beyond what was in front of her eyes to see the unseen things that God could do to reverse the situation in her school. She also spoke words of faith for months, strengthening her own faith as well as the faith of others. And when the situation was resolved, she was careful to give the credit to God, who had accomplished above and beyond what even she had anticipated.

If there's something in your life that seems impossible—something as big as a mountain standing between you and something you want or need—take that tiny little mustard-seed sized faith of yours and hand it over to God. Watch Him take it and make it grow. You'll end up with a supply of faith that's ready and waiting for the next big challenge that comes along. That's part of the beauty of exercising your faith—each time you place your faith in God, you store up a greater measure of faith, and the supply continues to grow.

I Will

Believe that God can enlarge my faith.   yes   no

Live by the definition of faith in Hebrews 11:1.   yes   no

Keep my faith in God intact no matter what I face
throughout the day.   yes   no

Realize that my faith will grow the more I
exercise it.   yes   no

Make sure that I speak words of faith and not
of doubt.   yes   no

Encourage others when their faith begins to weaken.   yes   no

Things to Do

☐ Read about the faith George Mueller had in God's provision (an online search will bring up numerous short biographical entries on him).

☐ Select one issue in your life that you need an exceptional amount of faith for and envision it as a mustard seed that you are planting in God's hands.

☐ Read about the great heroes of the faith in Hebrews 11.

☐ Oswald Chambers called faith "deliberate confidence in the character of God." Reflect on whether that definition applies to the way you exhibit your faith.

☐ Thank someone in your life who is an example to you of unwavering faith.

☐ Spend fifteen minutes writing down any memories of times when God has come through for you. (Keep that paper handy for times when your faith needs a boost.)

Things to Remember

Paul wrote: "I know whom I have believed and am persuaded that He is able to keep what I have committed to Him until that Day."

2 TIMOTHY 1:12 NKJV

Jesus' disciples said, "Now we are sure that You know all things, and have no need that anyone should question You. By this we believe that You came forth from God."

JOHN 16:30 NKJV

What is faith? It is the confident assurance that what we hope for is going to happen. It is the evidence of things we cannot yet see.
Hebrews 11:1 NLT

I know that my Redeemer lives, and He shall stand at last on the earth.

JOB 19:25 NKJV

Do you see that faith was working together with his works, and by works faith was made perfect?

JAMES 2:22 NKJV

Jesus said, "Let not your heart be troubled; you believe in God, believe also in Me."

JOHN 14:1 NKJV

You may believe that Jesus is the Christ, the Son of God, and that believing you may have life in His name.

JOHN 20:31 NKJV

The apostles said to the Lord, "Increase our faith."

LUKE 17:5 NKJV

In it the righteousness of God is revealed from faith to faith; as it is written, "The just shall live by faith."

ROMANS 1:17 NKJV

With the heart a man believes, resulting in righteousness, and with the mouth he confesses, resulting in salvation.

ROMANS 10:10 NASB

Paul wrote: "We live by faith, not by sight."

2 CORINTHIANS 5:7 NIV

Oh, GOD, here I am, your servant, your faithful servant: set me free for your service.

PSALM 116:16 THE MESSAGE

Faith is to believe what we do not see; and the reward of this faith is to see what we believe.

—SAINT AUGUSTINE

Faith is deliberate confidence in the character of God whose ways you may not understand at the time.

—OSWALD CHAMBERS

Sense of Humor

Lighten the Mood

Our mouth was filled with laughter, and our tongue with singing. Then they said among the nations, "The LORD has done great things for them."

—PSALM 126:2 NKJV

Jacob was one of those middle-school boys that just couldn't seem to keep his mouth closed. No matter what the situation, he had a comment, and that comment usually had the result of cracking up the entire class. He had legitimately earned the undisputed title of class clown.

In some of his classes, Jacob was considered a disruptive influence, and he spent a fair amount of his time in school in the guidance department. But one teacher, Mrs. Myers, never needed to send him to the office. That's because she shared his sense of humor and had the wisdom to channel it in a positive direction. She thought he was genuinely funny—to her, he wasn't a wisecracking kid but a witty student who had a way of defusing the tension that sometimes permeated the school day. Instead of crushing his sense of humor, she *planned* for it—and as a result, Jacob knew just how far he could go. Whenever he was in Mrs. Myers's class, he knew exactly when it was time to stop cracking jokes.

Positive humor has so many benefits that it's difficult to list them all. Medical studies have proven its effects on a person's physical health, while psychological studies have confirmed its benefits with regard to a person's emotional and mental well-being. And as Mrs. Myers's experience with Jacob revealed, it helps relieve the pressure of a stress-filled day and release the tension others are feeling.

For you as a teacher, allowing your sense of humor to come out in your teaching keeps your students interested and helps them to see your human side. Too many teachers feel they need to project a serious, let's-get-down-to-work-and-stay-there image, one that robs them of the joy God wants them to find in their work and robs the students of an opportunity to find a bit of pleasure in their school day.

Just remember that an attempt at humor that ends up being belittling or degrading to others is simply not funny—especially not to God. Laughing at others in a malicious way is mean-spirited and contrary to the Spirit of Christ. Laughing at yourself in a good-natured way, on the other hand, can have an amazingly healthy effect on your self-esteem. Keep your sense of humor close to the surface as you go through your day. It will lighten your load and lighten the moods of all those tension-filled people around you. Better yet, it just may help keep you, your students, and your colleagues emotionally and mentally sound.

I Will

Recognize the physical, emotional, and spiritual benefits of having a healthy sense of humor.

_____ yes   _____ no

Use appropriate humor in the classroom.

_____ yes   _____ no

See the evidence of God's sense of humor in my daily life.

_____ yes   _____ no

Learn to laugh at my foibles.

_____ yes   _____ no

Recognize the effectiveness of communicating truth through humor.

_____ yes   _____ no

React to frustration in a lighthearted way.

_____ yes   _____ no

Take genuine delight in my life and the people in it.

_____ yes   _____ no

Things to Do

☐ *Enter* laughter, *and similar words, into an online Bible search to discover how often it occurs in Scripture.*

☐ *Find an age-appropriate book of humorous illustrations to use in your classroom.*

☐ *Think back to a recent difficult situation that occurred in school and consider how humor could have changed that situation for the better.*

☐ *Browse through any of a number of sites devoted to the connection between humor and health, such as www.humorforyourhealth.com.*

☐ *Resurrect an activity you used to enjoy as a child and try it again this week, just for the fun of it.*

☐ *Go to a store and buy several funny cards so you'll have them on hand to send when someone needs cheering up.*

Things to Remember

A time to weep, and a time to laugh; a time to mourn, and a time to dance.

ECCLESIASTES 3:4 NKJV

A merry heart does good, like medicine, but a broken spirit dries the bones.

PROVERBS 17:22 NKJV

On your feet now—applaud GOD! Bring a gift of laughter, sing yourselves into his presence.

PSALM 100:1–2 THE MESSAGE

Those who went off with heavy hearts will come home laughing, with armloads of blessing.

PSALM 126:6 THE MESSAGE

David wrote: "I will be glad and rejoice in Your mercy, for You have considered my trouble; You have known my soul in adversities."

PSALM 31:7 NKJV

David wrote: "I'm whistling, laughing, and jumping for joy; I'm singing your song, High God."

PSALM 9:2 THE MESSAGE

Humor is by far the most significant activity of the human brain.

—EDWARD DE BONO

Humor is something that thrives between man's aspirations and his limitations. There is more logic in humor than in anything else. Because, you see, humor is truth.

—VICTOR BORGE

Complaining

Useless Grumbling

Do all things without complaining and disputing.
—Philippians 2:14 NKJV

As he reached to retrieve a pen from his jacket pocket, Phil's hand brushed against the index card on which his son had written the memory verse he was supposed to learn before church next week. Phil had placed it in his pocket after Sunday's service and forgotten to give it back to him. He pulled it out and looked at it so he could help his son begin memorizing it that night when he got home. "Do all things without complaining and disputing— Philippians 2:14," it read. His seven-year-old son would have that one mastered in no time.

Suddenly, though, Phil was taken aback by the words he read. *It's an easy enough verse to memorize,* he thought. *But it's hardly an easy one to master.* It was only noon, but already Phil had heard little but complaints all morning long—not just from his fifth-graders but also from the other teachers and the assistant principal. He was hard-pressed to remember a single positive comment anyone had made all morning; the answers his students gave to his questions in class could be considered neutral at best.

How long, he wondered, *could a person maintain a positive outlook on life if all he heard all day were complaints?*

Then Phil engaged in a bit of self-examination. What had his thoughts been like all morning? He had complained—whether verbally or mentally—about the coffee being too weak and the traffic being too slow, about the students who came in late and the students who came in unprepared. Even after reading his son's memory verse, he had complained because the pen he had reached for was out of ink. Well, if he was going to help his son *learn* that verse, he had to start by learning to *live* that verse himself.

For the next five days, Phil guarded his words and his thoughts. Every time he felt a complaint surface, he stopped himself; thanked God for freeing him from a complaining spirit; did what he could to change the situation; and got on with his life. Each night, he helped his son memorize the verse—and he never once complained about it. By Sunday, Phil felt like a new man.

If you want to feel like a new person, stop complaining. Stop even *thinking* about complaining. And as much as is possible, stop listening to complaining. If something is really bugging you, do what you can to correct the situation. Then get on with your life—the uncomplaining life God wants you to live.

I Will

Resist the urge to complain.

_____   _____

Cultivate an attitude of appreciation for the
wonderful life God has given me.

yes   no
_____   _____

Take action to resolve a situation rather than
complain about it.

yes   no
_____   _____

Discourage my students from complaining.

yes   no
_____   _____

Realize that things will not always go my way or
be to my liking.

yes   no
_____   _____

Find positive elements in every negative situation.

yes   no
_____   _____

Allow God's Spirit to give me a thankful heart.

yes   no
_____   _____

Things to Do

☐ *List every complaint you have about life. Laugh at what you've written and throw the list away.*

☐ *Read Exodus 16 to see how God feels about grumbling.*

☐ *Listen to the conversation in the teachers' lounge tomorrow and offer suggestions for resolving any situations the others are complaining about.*

☐ *Sit in your classroom and identify every nuisance, annoyance, and broken piece of equipment you've complained about, and decide what action you can take to rectify those problems.*

☐ *Read James 5:9 from* The Message *(on the facing page).*

☐ *For one day, keep a tally of every complaint you utter or are tempted to utter.*

Things to Remember

Do not say, "Why were the former days better than these?" For you do not inquire wisely concerning this.

ECCLESIASTES 7:10 NKJV

The people complained against Moses, saying, "What shall we drink?" So he cried out to the LORD, and the LORD showed him a tree. When he cast it into the waters, the waters were made sweet.

EXODUS 15:24–25 NKJV

Friends, don't complain about each other. A far greater complaint could be lodged against you, you know. The Judge is standing just around the corner.

JAMES 5:9 THE MESSAGE

These are grumblers, complainers, walking according to their own lusts; and they mouth great swelling words, flattering people to gain advantage.

JUDE 16 NKJV

Both bad and good things come by the command of the Most High God.

LAMENTATIONS 3:38 NCV

Martha was distracted with much serving, and she approached Him and said, "Lord, do You not care that my sister has left me to serve alone? Therefore tell her to help me."

LUKE 10:40 NKJV

Say and do something positive that will help the situation; it doesn't take any brains to complain.
—ROBERT A. COOK

Realize that if you have time to whine and complain about something then you have the time to do something about it.
—ANTHONY J. D'ANGELO

Praise

Raising Your Voice

Praise the LORD! Praise the LORD, O my soul! While I live I will praise the LORD; I will sing praises to my God while I have my being.

—PSALM 146:1–2 NKJV

At the start of the summer following his first year of teaching, Adam Walker had some serious thinking to do. The school year had been uneven at best—lots of highs, lots of lows, but mostly lots of nights questioning his suitability for the teaching profession. The son of two teachers, Adam considered himself better prepared for the challenges of teaching than most education majors he had met in college. But he wasn't prepared for the gradual erosion of his relationship with God during long and hectic days that too frequently had left him discouraged.

Before starting a summer job, Adam spent a much-needed week with his parents. As he had anticipated, these two veterans of a combined half century in the classroom listened to their son's concerns, asked questions, prayed with him and without him, offered theories about why he was discouraged, and listened some more. Of all the suggestions they made, there was one he could work on over the summer—praising God throughout the day. As

Adam's father had pointed out, his understanding of praise was incomplete; the only time he praised God was when things were going well. He had confused praise with thankfulness.

As Adam learned, God wants His people to praise Him no matter what happens, as David wrote in Psalm 34:1. In fact, David, who had a lifetime of opportunities to become discouraged and feel alienated from God, discovered the value of praising God and left a wealth of wisdom regarding praise in the many psalms he wrote. He pledged to praise God "every day . . . forever and ever" (Psalm 145:2 NKJV), "with my whole heart" (Psalm 138:1 NKJV). He praised God for who He is and not just for His works; he praised God even when the tide had turned against him.

When you immerse yourself in the book of Psalms, you discover the value of praising God all the time, in a variety of ways and circumstances, whether you feel like it or not. Praising God can readily become a habit in your life, one that you can practice throughout the day, no matter where you are. Whether you express yourself verbally, silently, in song, on paper, in your work or in your play, alone or with others, God is waiting for you to praise Him with your whole heart.

I Will

Realize that God wants me to praise Him.

yes _____ no _____

Remember to praise God for who He is and not just what He has done for me.

yes _____ no _____

Praise God for everything, whether good or bad.

yes _____ no _____

Learn how to praise God in different and creative ways: silently, vocally, through singing and writing, and so forth.

yes _____ no _____

Ask God to give me a heart of praise.

yes _____ no _____

Praise God even when I don't feel like it.

yes _____ no _____

Realize that nature also praises God (Luke 19:37–40).

yes _____ no _____

Things to Do

 Look up synonyms for the verb form of praise *in a thesaurus or at www.dictionary.com and select a half-dozen or so—such as* glorify, bless, worship—*to use in your praise of God.*

Schedule several praise breaks—even a minute of praising God will help—throughout each school day this week.

Choose several "praise" psalms—such as Psalm 9, 22, 30, 71—and pray them aloud to God.

Try to write your own psalms of praise to the Lord.

Visit a church radically different from your own and observe how the people praise God.

Sing a song of praise to God—even if you "can't" sing.

Things to Remember

All together now—applause for God!
Sing songs to the tune of his glory, set
glory to the rhythms of his praise!

PSALM 66:1–2 THE MESSAGE

I proclaim the name of the LORD:
Ascribe greatness to our God.

DEUTERONOMY 32:3 NKJV

Sing to Him, sing psalms to Him; talk of
all His wondrous works!

PSALM 105:2 NKJV

Praise the LORD from the heavens; praise
Him in the heights! Praise Him, all His
angels; praise Him, all His hosts! Praise
Him, sun and moon; praise Him, all
you stars of light!

PSALM 148:1–3 NKJV

I will praise the Lord no matter what
happens. I will constantly speak of his
glories and grace.

PSALM 34:1 TLB

O LORD, I will praise you with all my
heart, and tell everyone about the
marvelous things you do.

PSALM 9:1 TLB

To say "well done"
to any bit of good
work is to take
hold of the powers
which have made
the effort and
strengthen them
beyond our
knowledge.

—PHILLIPS BROOKS

We increase
whatever we praise.
The whole creation
responds to praise,
and is glad.

—CHARLES FILLMORE

Integrity

Professional Conduct

Paul wrote: "We are proud that our conscience is clear. We are proud of the way that we have lived in this world. We have lived with a God-given holiness and sincerity, especially toward you. It was not by human wisdom that we have lived but by God's kindness."

—2 Corinthians 1:12 GOD'S WORD

Three years ago, Christine Pelton was a young biology teacher relatively unknown on a professional level outside her rural Kansas school district. But all that changed during the 2001–2002 school year, when Pelton failed twenty-eight of her students—one-fifth of the total number of students in her classes—for cheating on their semester projects by plagiarizing from material found on the Internet. The previous semester, Pelton had also failed a number of students for the same offense.

This time, though, things were different. The parents of the students accused of cheating protested to the board of education, some indicating that their children didn't realize they had plagiarized, most arguing that a failing grade was too severe a punishment. The board ordered Pelton to change the grades so all twenty-eight students would pass the course—despite a course contract each student had signed acknowledging that cheating would result in a failing grade. Students who had legitimately earned high grades would receive lower grades under the revised structure.

Pelton resigned immediately, and a number of other teachers in the district pledged to do the same at the end of the school year. Their authority in the classroom had been eroded, but more importantly, so had their commitment to a high standard of integrity on the part of both the students and the teachers. So widespread was the fallout from this incident in a small Midwest town that CBS's *48 Hours* dedicated an entire segment to Pelton's case and others similar to hers.

One of the hallmarks of integrity is living in a way that is consistent with a moral or ethical code to which you adhere. Consistency is a key, and its absence in Pelton's case is glaringly obvious. Pelton had been consistent in following through with the moral standard she had created in her classroom and which her students had agreed to follow. But when the students failed to follow it—and their parents protested—the school board that had supported Pelton's standards in previous years lost any claim to integrity by issuing a directive that was inconsistent with those standards and with their prior actions.

As a teacher, you have abundant opportunities to demonstrate integrity in the classroom, though, as Pelton discovered, they may not always be appreciated. As she and her colleagues also discovered, maintaining integrity is essential to maintaining authority. But even more important is maintaining a clear conscience before God and others. By living in a way that remained consistent with her moral code, Christine Pelton gave her students and the community the priceless example of a person who would not violate that code regardless of the cost.

In many cases, situations that threaten your integrity will not be so clear-cut. Nor will the consequences be that severe. Still, those small areas in which you are tempted to compromise and violate your moral code are just as important as the larger threats, because each small victory builds on previous ones to create a lifestyle of consistency. When the bigger temptations come, you have a history of victories that stand as a testimony to the value of living a life of integrity.

Adherence to a moral code, however, doesn't mean you can't extend grace when that's what is called for. A life of integrity is not a life of slavish submission to a list of rules; it's living in a way that is honorable and trustworthy, dependable and truthful, principled and just. And it's living in a way that is gracious. You can extend grace to an offender in your classroom without jeopardizing your integrity—any time the circumstances and your own conscience allow you to. God's Spirit will give the peace and confidence of knowing that you are acting appropriately.

Your moral code of integrity can be one you've actually written—or it can simply be the Word of God written on your heart. You can't find a better measure for your character than the moral standards that permeate the Bible. Reading the Word of God, understanding its lessons on right living, and applying the truths you learn to your own life will develop within you a standard of integrity that no one has been able to improve on in two thousand years.

I Will

Demonstrate integrity in the way I live.

yes _____ no _____

Follow God's guidance in the moral decisions I must make.

yes _____ no _____

Maintain a clear conscience.

yes _____ no _____

Recognize the God-given opportunities I have to model integrity for others.

yes _____ no _____

Be aboveboard in all of my personal and professional relationships.

yes _____ no _____

Trust God to keep my motives pure and my actions honorable.

yes _____ no _____

Things to Do

☐ *Memorize at least two of the accompanying verses on integrity.*

☐ *Use a recent incident in the classroom involving cheating or dishonesty as a springboard to a lesson on character.*

☐ *Read Luke 16:10–15, in which Jesus discusses the importance of maintaining integrity in even the smallest matters.*

☐ *Come up with a ready response to use if a colleague tries to lure you into an unethical professional situation.*

☐ *Think of a recent occasion in which you acted in a less-than-honorable way and reflect on how the situation would have turned out had you acted with greater integrity.*

☐ *Write, call, or e-mail someone who has demonstrated integrity in a difficult situation, expressing your admiration for him or her.*

Things to Remember

You are witnesses, and God also, how devoutly and justly and blamelessly we behaved ourselves among you who believe.

1 THESSALONIANS 2:10 NKJV

He who walks with integrity walks securely, but he who perverts his ways will become known.

PROVERBS 10:9 NKJV

*The integrity of good people creates
a safe place for living.*
Proverbs 14:32 THE MESSAGE

The righteous man walks in his integrity; his children are blessed after him.

PROVERBS 20:7 NKJV

As for me, You uphold me in my integrity, and set me before Your face forever.

PSALM 41:12 NKJV

Exhort the young men to be sober-minded, in all things showing yourself to be a pattern of good works.

TITUS 2:6–7 NKJV

Let integrity and uprightness preserve me, for I wait for You.

PSALM 25:21 NKJV

They show that in their hearts they know what is right and wrong, just as the law commands. And they show this by their consciences. Sometimes their thoughts tell them they did wrong, and sometimes their thoughts tell them they did right.

ROMANS 2:15 NCV

Create in me a clean heart, O God, and renew a steadfast spirit within me.

PSALM 51:10 NKJV

Lord, you have examined me and know all about me. You know when I sit down and when I get up. You know my thoughts before I think them.

PSALM 139:1–2 NCV

Lo, God will not reject [a man of] integrity, nor will He support the evildoers.

JOB 8:20 NASB

Vindicate me, O LORD, for I have walked in my integrity, and I have trusted in the LORD without wavering.

PSALM 26:1 NASB

Nothing more completely baffles one who is full of tricks and duplicity than straight-forward and simple integrity in another.

—CHARLES CALEB COLTON

Integrity is what we do, what we say, and what we say we do.

—DON GALER

Peace

Tranquility Amid Turmoil

Jesus said, "Peace I leave with you, My peace I give to you; not as the world gives do I give to you. Let not your heart be troubled, neither let it be afraid."

—JOHN 14:27 NKJV

Dolores Hartnett sat in church listening to Pastor Robinson preach about the "peace that passes understanding." A sense of longing seemed to flood her entire being; she had once known that kind of peace and had even counseled others on how to find the serenity that so often eluded twenty-first-century Americans. But now, as a regional director for the state NEA chapter, Mrs. Hartnett spent an inordinate amount of her time immersed in problems she couldn't solve, issues she couldn't resolve, and bickering she couldn't control. All that had robbed her of her peace.

One point in particular that Pastor Robinson made in his sermon nagged at Mrs. Hartnett for the rest of the day. "To find peace," he quipped, "you have to resign as manager of the universe; there's only one qualified candidate for that position, and it's not you." That comment resonated with Dolores. She was a "fixer" and always had been, which is one of the primary reasons she was selected to be a regional director. She was a woman known for getting things done. Less known was her inability to accept the fact that she had difficulty coming to terms with the fact that she couldn't fix it all.

That night, Dolores sat down with her Bible and a topical Bible, one that lists every verse on a specific topic—in this case, inner peace or spiritual peace. She meditatively read verse after verse, stopping to reflect on those that seemed to have the greatest personal meaning to her and copying those in a notebook she always kept with her Bible. Hours passed, and so did the turmoil that had become all too familiar to her spirit. To her surprise, she had filled multiple pages of her notebook with verses, prayers, and marginal notes identifying the specific aspects of her life and her work that she had allowed to take the place of the peace of God.

Too often, people desire peace but do little to attain it. There's no question that God can and does supernaturally provide a sense of peace at times, especially in the midst of a crisis or disaster. But as Mrs. Hartnett discovered, you can also find peace through a number of spiritual activities, several of which she engaged in at one sitting: Bible reading, prayer, meditation and reflection, and journaling. Couple those activities with consciously and intentionally turning control of your universe back to God—Mrs. Hartnett's final activity before she went to bed that night—and you'll find yourself the grateful recipient of the peace Jesus promised He would give to you.

I Will

Accept peace as both a promise and a gift
from God.

yes   _no_

Give to God those things that are stressful to me
and rob me of my peace.

yes   _no_

Learn from those people who have discovered how
to live peaceful lives in a tumultuous world.

yes   _no_

Realize that my choices may be responsible for the
loss of peace in my life.

yes   _no_

Believe that God is in control and knows what He is
doing in the world.

yes   _no_

Practice biblical meditation.

yes   _no_

Things to Do

 Post the word peace *in your classroom where you can see it; let it remind you to turn your heart and thoughts toward God throughout the day.*

Write out Philippians 4:7 on an index card and carry it with you until you have it memorized.

Read John 14:25–27 and reflect on the peace Jesus gives in contrast to the kind of peace the world offers.

List everything that you believe stands between you and the peace you crave; ask God to show you how to handle those obstacles.

Create a Bible study on peace or purchase one—such as Max Lucado's Joy in the Morning: Studies on Peace.

Be open and vulnerable to another person—a friend or a counselor— about the lack of peace in your life.

Things to Remember

The LORD gives strength to his people;
the LORD blesses his people with peace.

PSALM 29:11 NCV

Great peace have those who love Your
law, and nothing causes them to
stumble.

PSALM 119:165 NKJV

Acquaint yourself with Him, and be at
peace; thereby good will come to you.

JOB 22:21 NKJV

Let the peace of God rule in your hearts,
to which also you were called in one
body; and be thankful.

COLOSSIANS 3:15 NKJV

The peace of God, which surpasses all
understanding, will guard your hearts
and minds through Christ Jesus.

PHILIPPIANS 4:7 NKJV

Grace to you and peace from God our
Father and the Lord Jesus Christ.

1 CORINTHIANS 1:3 NKJV

Peace is not
something you wish
for; it's something
you make, some-
thing you do,
something you are,
and something you
give away.

—ROBERT FULGHUM

First keep peace
with yourself, then
you can also bring
peace to others.

—THOMAS à KEMPIS

Seeking Wisdom

Priceless Instruction

My instruction is far more valuable than silver or gold. For the value of wisdom is far above rubies; nothing can be compared with it.

—Proverbs 8:10–11 TLB

Cathy Taylor was the kind of teacher every district loved. Energetic, enthusiastic, determined to do everything in her power to make the school and the classroom a better place to be. Daily she incorporated innovative and creative elements into her lessons; nightly she devoured teaching magazines and journals and surfed the Internet for even more information that would help her become a better teacher. She spent her summers taking courses in her pursuit of master's degrees in education and biology, her subject area.

No question about it—when it came to the pursuit of knowledge and the ability to impart that knowledge in a way her middle-school students could understand, Cathy Taylor was a dream teacher. With time, though, the same set of recurring problems emerged from her classroom, such as poorly handled disciplinary problems and students distraught over the way she had treated them. It seems that with all of her knowledge, Miss Taylor had not acquired very much wisdom.

Wisdom is markedly different from knowledge, and so is the process of acquiring it. You can obtain knowledge from books or lectures, as well as a variety of other media, because knowledge is essentially information. Wisdom, on the other hand, encompasses a range of qualities—insight, discernment, judgment, perception, and understanding—that you would be hard-pressed to acquire the same way you acquire knowledge. Instead, God has provided a more personal means of granting you the wisdom you seek:

Prayer: Solomon asked for wisdom, and God made him the wisest man on earth in his time. The book of James encourages believers to specifically ask for wisdom and promises that God will generously give it to you. The wisdom He gives may be in the form of specific help in handling an immediate problem, or gradual insight into the way life works—and the way God intended it to work—over a long period of time. No one, not even Solomon, can be said to have acquired all the wisdom available from God. God gives people the measure of wisdom they need.

Scripture: Within the Bible is a set of books known collectively as the wisdom books: Job, Psalms, Proverbs, Ecclesiastes, and Song of Solomon. There's plenty of wisdom in the other books, of course, but these five books offer an intensive, focused perspective on life from God's point of view. Proverbs in particular addresses moral and ethical behavior and offers a deep understanding of human nature. Additionally, the words of Jesus in the Gospels and the insight offered through the Epistles to the early church in the New Testament provide insight into a better way to live, from the perspective of the new covenant, the one that was established with the resurrection of Jesus.

Personal experience: If you pay careful and close attention to the experiences you have had in your life, and the experiences you have had with God, you can be well on your way toward acquiring the kind of wisdom you can apply to future experiences. And you can be in a strong position to offer counsel to others who desperately need the wisdom that comes from God rather than the worldly wisdom that is based largely on changeable opinion rather than eternal truth.

Others' experiences: Other people can be invaluable in imparting wisdom to you. Whether it's through one-on-one counseling with a Christian mentor or pastor, or through the abundance of conferences, tapes, and sermons available to you, or through the writings of the great thinkers in the history of Christianity, you can acquire a great deal of wisdom by availing yourself of the multitude of resources that recount the experiences other people have had with God that have given them greater insight into themselves, other people, and God Himself. And that, in turn, has helped them handle life and its many challenges in a far wiser way.

You can have a great deal of knowledge and still suffer from a remarkable lack of wisdom, just like Mrs. Taylor. Or you can start today and begin accumulating a storehouse of wisdom, just by asking God for it and allowing Him to speak to you through the Bible, your own experiences, and the experiences of others. It's a gift, and it's yours for the asking.

I Will

Seek the wisdom that comes from God.   _____ yes   _____ no

Place a higher value on wisdom than the value I place on silver or gold or gemstones.   _____ yes   _____ no

Realize that every time I read the Bible I have the opportunity to acquire greater wisdom.   _____ yes   _____ no

Understand the value of learning from those who are wiser than I am.   _____ yes   _____ no

Recognize mistakes and failures as opportunities to grow in wisdom.   _____ yes   _____ no

Expect spiritual growth as I draw on the wisdom God provides.   _____ yes   _____ no

Things to Do

☐ *Reflect on your day (or yesterday, if you're reading this in the morning) and take note of the snippets of wisdom you heard or read during the course of the day.*

☐ *Analyze a current world situation or political issue in light of God's wisdom, contrasting it with worldly wisdom.*

☐ *Memorize James 1:5 and ask God to give you the wisdom He promises in that verse.*

☐ *Ask God to give you wisdom in handling the more challenging students in your class.*

☐ *Use a concordance to find all the references to wisdom in the book of Proverbs, and choose several passages to memorize.*

☐ *Thank God for every bit of wisdom He has given you.*

Things to Remember

The fear of the LORD is the beginning of wisdom; a good understanding have all those who do His commandments. His praise endures forever.

PSALM 111:10 NKJV

Happy is the person who finds wisdom, the one who gets understanding. Wisdom is worth more than silver; it brings more profit than gold. Wisdom is more precious than rubies; nothing you could want is equal to it.

PROVERBS 3:13–15 NCV

If any of you lack wisdom, you should pray to God, who will give it to you; because God gives generously and graciously to all.
James 1:5 GNT

The law of the LORD is perfect, restoring the soul; the testimony of the LORD is sure, making wise the simple.

PSALM 19:7 NASB

The fear of the LORD is the beginning of wisdom, and the knowledge of the Holy One is understanding.

PROVERBS 9:10 NKJV

Don't fool yourselves. Suppose some of you think you are wise by the standards of the world. Then you should become a "fool" so that you can become wise. The wisdom of this world is foolishness in God's eyes. It is written, "God catches wise people in their own tricks."

1 CORINTHIANS 3:18–19 NIrV

The words of good people are wise, and they are always fair.

PSALM 37:30 GNT

In the same way, wisdom is pleasing to you. If you find it, you have hope for the future, and your wishes will come true.

PROVERBS 24:14 NCV

The wisdom from above is first pure, then peaceable, gentle, reasonable, full of mercy and good fruits, unwavering, without hypocrisy.

JAMES 3:17 NASB

Knowledge comes, but wisdom lingers.

—CALVIN COOLIDGE

You desire truth in the innermost being, and in the hidden part You will make me know wisdom.

PSALM 51:6 NASB

He who exercises wisdom exercises the knowledge which is about God.

—EPICTETUS

The Lord gives wisdom; from his mouth come knowledge and understanding.

PROVERBS 2:6 NRSV

True wisdom and real power belong to God; from him we learn how to live, and also what to live for.

JOB 12:13 THE MESSAGE

Criticism

Critical Thinking

Let us not judge one another anymore, but rather resolve this, not to put a stumbling block or a cause to fall in our brother's way.
—ROMANS 14:13 NKJV

Sondra Barker listened intently as a highly respected teacher gave the keynote address at the state teachers' convention. This wasn't at all what she had expected to hear; most years, the keynoter kept to an unwritten rule and opened the convention with little more than a cheerleading session sprinkled with a few politically correct comments intended to get the group fired up over an issue they pretty much all agreed on anyway. The speaker this year, though, was challenging the teachers to a higher standard of behavior both in and out of the classroom, and right now, she was chastising her colleagues for criticizing each other as well as the students and their parents, the administration in their schools, the school boards, and the state and national leadership in various teachers' organizations.

The speaker's remarks gave her pause. Mrs. Barker had recently borne the brunt of some very ugly and critical remarks made by one or two colleagues—not teachers she had a whole lot of respect for, but still, their comments had prompted her to retaliate by criticizing them. She had been so disappointed in herself; that was not like her, but the atmosphere at the school had become so charged with criticism that she had allowed herself to be influenced by it.

Once she returned home from the conference and had some time to herself, Mrs. Barker began a process of intentional change first by asking God to forgive her and to replace her critical spirit with a heart of compassion. Then she began listing, as quickly as the thought came to her, everything she had been critical of in the recent past, whether she had verbalized the criticism or not. After just a few minutes of writing, she knew this was a much bigger problem area for her than she had previously admitted. She worked her way through the list, asking God to not only forgive her but also make amends to those people she had offended with her critical nature. Finally, she found a few pertinent verses on controlling one's thoughts and speech, and copied them to carry with her so she could memorize them.

Controlling your critical nature is not something that happens in some supernatural or miraculous way. It takes a fair amount of work and discipline and intentional action, as well as a heavy dose of dependence on God. But you can do it, and God will be faithful to replace your critical nature with one that is saturated with understanding and compassion toward others.

I Will

Focus on what I need to change about myself rather than what I think others need to change.

yes _____ no _____

Trust God to change my negative attitude.

yes _____ no _____

Develop a compassionate and loving attitude toward others.

yes _____ no _____

Turn my critical thoughts into positive and helpful actions.

yes _____ no _____

Allow God's Spirit to have control over my thought life.

yes _____ no _____

Be as gracious and understanding toward other people as I would want them to be toward me.

yes _____ no _____

Things to Do

☐ *Choose one project or program at school that you've been critical of and list the action steps you could take to benefit the situation.*

☐ *Think of the person you've had the most critical thoughts about lately, and place that person's name at the very top of your prayer list.*

☐ *Read Matthew 7:1–12 and meditate on what Jesus said about criticism.*

☐ *Reflect on how quickly your critical nature would be transformed if you truly loved other people the way God wants you to.*

☐ *Ask forgiveness from anyone you have criticized lately.*

☐ *Forgive yourself for being so self-critical—and resolve to stop putting yourself down.*

Things to Remember

Jesus said, "Judge not, and you shall not be judged. Condemn not, and you shall not be condemned. Forgive, and you will be forgiven."

LUKE 6:37 NKJV

You can offer no excuse, O man, whoever indulges in judging; for by passing judgment on another you condemn yourself, since you, who are passing judgment practice the same things.

ROMANS 2:1 MLB

Tell them not to speak evil of anyone, but to be peaceful and friendly, and always to show a gentle attitude toward everyone.

TITUS 3:2 GNT

Jesus said, "Blessed are you when men hate you, and when they exclude you, and revile you, and cast out your name as evil, for the Son of Man's sake."

LUKE 6:22 NKJV

My brothers and sisters, don't speak against one another. Anyone who speaks against another believer speaks against the law. And anyone who judges another believer judges the law. When you judge the law, you are not keeping it.

JAMES 4:11 NIrV

The rule in carving holds good as to criticism; never cut with a knife what you can cut with a spoon.

—CHARLES BUXTON

If evil be spoken of you and it be true, correct yourself, if it be a lie, laugh at it.

—EPICTETUS

Humility

Like a Little Child

Jesus said, "Whoever humbles himself as this little child is the greatest in the kingdom of heaven."
—MATTHEW 18:4 NKJV

The humble teacher was amassing quite a following, much to the dismay of those teachers who considered themselves far more learned and sophisticated than this undereducated fellow would ever be. Who did he think he was, coming into their district and introducing all these new ideas that made people question what they had been taught their whole lives? Some of the professional teachers wanted to run him out of town, while others harbored far more sinister thoughts about what to do with him. Most, though, just hoped he'd fade off into oblivion and quit making trouble for them.

It's been two thousand years, and Jesus is still nowhere near fading off into oblivion. What those professional teachers—the Pharisees—failed to realize was that one of the qualities that made Jesus so attractive to His followers was His humility, a quality that was in short supply among the religious leadership at the time. Jesus had every right to bully His way into the lives of the people. He was, after all,

God Himself, and He could have seen His mission as a crusade to whip the people into shape once and for all. But no. He clothed Himself in *humility*—a word related to humus, a rich component of soil. Jesus became earthy and grounded for our sake. His life on earth was a lowly one compared to all He left behind with the Father. He is the perfect example of humility (see Philippians 2:6–8).

The Pharisees, on the other hand, were the very definition of pride. Their arrogance, self-importance, and haughty demeanor was well known and well documented by the Gospel writers. Those people who paid any attention to them at all feared them and the power they wielded over their lives. At the word of a Pharisee, a person could be branded with some sin and therefore harmed for life. They may have been erudite, but these teachers never demonstrated humility.

Humble people give God and others the credit for the success in their lives. They put other people first and guide them toward the limelight while they back away. They never browbeat or make demands of other people, even if they are in a position to. Humble people are the servant leaders of the world.

Follow Jesus' example and take on the characteristics of the humble teacher that He was. Be a servant leader in your classroom and in your school—clothed in humility, grounded in God, just like Jesus.

I Will

Realize that God gives grace to the humble. _____ yes _____ no

Ask God to reveal the areas of pride in my life. _____ yes _____ no

Discover what true humility is. _____ yes _____ no

Demonstrate humility in my relationships
with others. _____ yes _____ no

Imitate Christ's example of humility. _____ yes _____ no

Give the glory and honor and credit for my
success to God. _____ yes _____ no

Put others first. _____ yes _____ no

Things to Do

☐ *Perform a random act of humility by swallowing your pride and doing a good, anonymous deed for someone you aren't particularly fond of.*

☐ *Participate in a foot-washing ceremony (usually held on Maunday Thursday before Easter); schedule it on your calendar.*

☐ *List areas of pride in your life, confess them to God, accept His forgiveness, and tear up the list.*

☐ *Come up with some practical ways you can demonstrate humility toward difficult colleagues.*

☐ *Reflect on Monica Baldwin's comment on humility and apply its wisdom to your life.*

☐ *Assess the way you can display humility before your students while maintaining your authority.*

Things to Remember

All of you be submissive to one another, and be clothed with humility, for "God resists the proud, but gives grace to the humble."

1 PETER 5:5 NKJV

Humble yourselves under the mighty hand of God, that He may exalt you in due time.

1 PETER 5:6 NKJV

Jesus said, "Whoever exalts himself will be humbled, and he who humbles himself will be exalted."

MATTHEW 23:12 NKJV

Before destruction the heart of a man is haughty, and before honor is humility.

PROVERBS 18:12 NKJV

By humility and the fear of the LORD are riches and honor and life.

PROVERBS 22:4 NKJV

David wrote: "My soul shall make its boast in the LORD; the humble shall hear of it and be glad."

PSALM 34:2 NKJV

What makes humility so desirable is the marvelous thing it does to us; it creates in us a capacity for the closest possible intimacy with God.

—MONICA BALDWIN

Many people believe that humility is the opposite of pride, when, in fact, it is a point of equilibrium. The opposite of pride is actually a lack of self-esteem. A humble person is totally different from a person who cannot recognize and appreciate himself as part of this world's marvels.

—RABINO NILTON BONDER

Work

God in the Classroom

Do your work with enthusiasm. Work as if you were serving the Lord, not as if you were serving only men and women.
—EPHESIANS 6:7 NCV

When Jeremy's wife received a long-awaited promotion, it came with the condition that she would transfer to her law firm's Chicago office. Relocating from a small town in the Bible belt to a major city would be a challenge, but the couple knew God had orchestrated the move. Sandra's mother's health was failing, and now they would be living less than an hour's drive from her.

Finding a job teaching seventh-grade history in Chicago proved to be one of the easiest aspects of the move. Jeremy settled in to his new position readily enough, but he missed the fellowship he had enjoyed with the teachers and staff he had left behind in Tennessee. Nearly all were Christians, and they had continually encouraged each other to remember that ultimately they were working for God.

In Chicago, Jeremy found it harder to maintain that perspective. His particular school had been threatened with a lawsuit for including a religious song in the annual holiday concert, and everyone, it seemed, was skittish about discussing religion on any level—especially on a personal faith level. By the end of the school year, Jeremy had become so discouraged that he considered pursuing another vocation entirely. His first step in that direction took him back to Tennessee for a greatly needed extended visit with Tom, an old friend and teaching mentor at his previous school.

Tom listened carefully as Jeremy described several options he was considering and listed the reasons he felt he should leave the teaching profession. Clearly, Jeremy's main problem was that he had lost his sense of mission by allowing the fearful atmosphere at his new school to erode his understanding of God's purpose for his life. As a result, his work lacked purpose. He had become jaded, and he no longer felt useful. Over the next several days, Tom reminded Jeremy of some of the details of his spiritual history, how he had been called to teach and how he had been deeply committed to teaching.

Driving back to Chicago following his week-long vacation, Jeremy replayed one comment Tom made over and over again in his mind: *God is in your classroom, Jeremy, whether the school board or the community acknowledges that fact or not. You have been filled with God's Spirit, and where you go, He goes.* Just as he had when they were coworkers, Tom had reminded Jeremy once again that ultimately, he was working for God. In the fall, Jeremy returned to school with a renewed passion for teaching and a renewed sense of purpose regarding his life's work

If you are likewise filled with the Spirit of God, then you can be assured that God is in your classroom as well. You can also be assured that if you "work as if you were serving the Lord, not as if you were serving only men and women," you can rekindle the passion for teaching that may have dimmed with the passing of time or the changing of circumstances. Recall your own spiritual history, especially if God was a part of your initial decision to pursue a teaching career.

If you're still dissatisfied—or if your decision to become a teacher was made without God's input—it may be that God is calling you to spend some concentrated time reflecting on your job in light of His purpose for your life. Through prayer and counsel with a mature Christian, identify what that purpose is and make sure that your chosen profession lines up with that purpose. It could be that God is steering you in a different direction—or it could be that you are exactly where He wants you to be, but your thinking and your attitude toward your job need to be transformed. No one can decide that for you; God's peace will confirm that you've made the right decision.

Even the best jobs—and thank God if yours is one of them—can stand a bit of improvement now and then to keep them fresh and interesting. If you're convinced you're where God wants you to be, maybe you just need to shake things up a bit by injecting new life into your workday and your routines. Consciously bring God into your classroom with you, and allow Him to infuse His life into your work.

I Will

Dedicate my work life to God. yes _____ no _____

Maintain a positive attitude toward my job. yes _____ no _____

Work as if God were my immediate supervisor. yes _____ no _____

Establish excellence as the ultimate standard for the work I do. yes _____ no _____

Believe that God will bless my work, my students, and my colleagues. yes _____ no _____

Realize that the work I do helps me to grow in character. yes _____ no _____

Things to Do

 Spend some focused time reflecting on your level of satisfaction with your current job and pray specifically about what you have discovered.

Come up with at least three action steps you can take to improve your situation at work.

Ask several teachers for recommendations on courses or seminars on developing your professional skills.

Write down your career goals, after spending time in prayer about your future as a teacher.

Recall the factors that led you into teaching and determine if you would make the same decision if you were entering the workforce today.

Create a "Top Ten Things I Love About Teaching" list—and post it in a prominent place.

Things to Remember

Whether we feast or fast, it's up to God. God may give wisdom and knowledge and joy to his favorites, but sinners are assigned a life of hard labor, and end up turning their wages over to God's favorites. Nothing but smoke—and spitting into the wind.

ECCLESIASTES 2:25–26 THE MESSAGE

Men and women go out to work, busy at their jobs until evening.

PSALM 104:23 THE MESSAGE

Paul wrote: "Even when we were with you, we commanded you this: If anyone will not work, neither shall he eat."
2 Thessalonians 3:10 NKJV

The psalmist wrote: "He commanded Joseph to keep this day so we'd never forget what he did in Egypt. I hear this most gentle whisper from One I never guessed would speak to me: 'I took the world off your shoulders, freed you from a life of hard labor. You called to me in your pain; I got you out of a bad place. I answered you from where the thunder hides, I proved you at Meribah Fountain.' "

PSALM 81:5–7 THE MESSAGE

Remain in the same house, eating and drinking such things as they give, for the laborer is worthy of his wages. Do not go from house to house.

LUKE 10:7 NKJV

You will eat the fruit of your labor;
blessings and prosperity will be yours.

PSALM 128:2 NIV

Paul wrote: "Every time we think of you,
we thank God for you. Day and night
you're in our prayers as we call to mind
your work of faith, your labor of love,
and your patience of hope in following
our Master, Jesus Christ, before God our
Father."

1 THESSALONIANS 1:2–3 THE MESSAGE

Unless the LORD builds the house, its
builders labor in vain. Unless the LORD
watches over the city, the watchmen
stand guard in vain.

PSALM 127:1 NIV

God said: "Six days you shall labor, but
on the seventh day you shall rest; even
during the plowing season and harvest
you must rest."

EXODUS 34:21 NIV

He brings our work to a stop; he shows
us what he can do.

JOB 37:7 GNT

Whatever your hand finds to do, do it
with your might; for there is no work or
device or knowledge or wisdom in the
grave where you are going.

ECCLESIASTES 9:10 NKJV

**Every calling is
great when greatly
pursued.**
—OLIVER WENDELL
HOLMES

**Work joyfully and
peacefully, knowing
that right thoughts
and right efforts
will inevitably
bring about right
results.**
—JAMES ALLEN

Love

The Greatest of These

Love never stops being patient, never stops believing, never stops hoping, never gives up.

—1 Corinthians 13:7 God's word

A classic description of Christian love is found in 1 Corinthians 13, one of the best-loved sections in the Bible. In fact, you may be so familiar with it that you haven't even thought to apply its truth to your job. But take a look at how just one verse in the chapter—verse 7— relates to some of your toughest challenges as a teacher.

Love never stops being patient. This is a big one, isn't it? How many times in the course of a day are you tempted to lose your patience? You will likely lose your patience on occasion, but your big-picture patience—your even-tempered endurance over the long haul—is what will see you through each school year. It all depends on your attitude: If you're simply gritting your teeth and holding back a torrent of pent-up frustration, you won't make it. But if you genuinely love your students as God loves them, you'll not only endure to the end, but also do so joyfully.

Love never stops believing. You can make a difference in your students' lives, as long as you believe in them and in

God's behind-the-scenes activity in their lives. By loving them with the power that God has given you, you help open their hearts to God's love and to an awareness of His purpose for their lives. Don't ever stop believing.

Love never stops hoping. That means having faith in the unseen—the hidden potential of each student and each colleague that's waiting to be revealed. Your loving attitude confirms your faith in their potential and can help them hold on to their hopes and their dreams for the future.

Love never gives up. Monica was the mother of one of the town's best-known degenerates. Day after day, night after night, she prayed that God would grab hold of his life and transform him into the man she knew he could be. She never gave up— and her prayers were answered. For a thousand years, her son—now known as Saint Augustine—has been revered as one of the church's greatest theologians. Your persistent, relentless prayers for your students could have far-reaching consequences.

Read through the rest of the chapter, applying its definition of love to your unique situation. God's love is the only love that is eternal. By drawing on His love, and extending it to others in your life—students, colleagues, friends, family members—your impact on their lives may live on throughout eternity.

I Will

Love God with all my heart, soul, and strength.   yes ___   no ___

Learn how to love myself.   yes ___   no ___

Love others as I love myself.   yes ___   no ___

Discover appropriate ways to extend love to my students.   yes ___   no ___

Thank God for His love for me.   yes ___   no ___

Give love to others without expecting love in return.   yes ___   no ___

Realize that I can decide to love even when I don't feel like it.   yes ___   no ___

Things to Do

☐ *Reflect on Nick Richardson's quotation on the facing page and how you can apply its truth to your relationships.*

☐ *Brainstorm with another Christian teacher about appropriate ways you can show your students that you love them with the love of God.*

☐ *List the various ways you've demonstrated love toward others in the past and determine which have been the most effective.*

☐ *Identify your most difficult colleague and ask God for creative means and opportunities to love that person in a practical way.*

☐ *Come up with your own definitions of various kinds of love: spiritual love, romantic love, love for humanity.*

☐ *Set aside some uninterrupted time and ask God to show you specific ways you can be more loving toward others.*

Things to Remember

Love is patient. Love is kind. It does not want what belongs to others. It does not brag. It is not proud.

1 CORINTHIANS 13:4 NIrV

John wrote: "We have known and believed the love that God has for us. God is love."

1 JOHN 4:16 NKJV

Owe no one anything except to love one another.

ROMANS 13:8 NKJV

The three most important things to have are faith, hope and love. But the greatest of them is love.

1 CORINTHIANS 13:13 NIrV

Watch over your heart with all diligence, for from it flow the springs of life.

PROVERBS 4:23 NASB

Love is eternal. There are inspired messages, but they are temporary; there are gifts of speaking in strange tongues, but they will cease; there is knowledge, but it will pass.

1 CORINTHIANS 13:8 GNT

Love talked about is easily turned aside, but love demonstrated is irresistible.

—STAN MOONEYHAM

Love is what is left in a relationship after all the selfishness is taken out.

—NICK RICHARDSON

Anxiety

Stress Reduction

Be anxious for nothing, but in everything by prayer and supplication, with thanksgiving, let your requests be made known to God.

—PHILIPPIANS 4:6 NKJV

Every summer since becoming a teacher, Mrs. Carlson had dedicated her time to revamping all her lesson plans for the coming year. She never wanted her teaching to become stale, and she never wanted to be known as a boring teacher. For five years in a row, she had completely reworked her lessons—and for five years in a row, the stress on her had accumulated until it finally reached the breaking point. It was time to seek professional help from a counselor who worked with teachers.

After several meetings in which Mrs. Carlson essentially described the multitude of stresses on her life, the counselor struck pay dirt when Mrs. Carlson offhandedly mentioned the added stress of redoing her lesson plans every summer. "You're reinventing the wheel year after year," he said to her. "There's no need for that. Not only that, having to teach new lessons every day for five years has placed you in a chronic state of anxiety. You now have five years' worth of lesson plans—stop creating new ones. When you feel the need to freshen those up, change 20 percent of the material one year, another 20 percent the following year, and so on. They'll never get stale, and you'll reduce your stress immeasurably."

Like Mrs. Carlson, some teachers get in the habit of reinventing the wheel because they're afraid that their lessons or their teaching style will become tired and dated. That's a valid concern, but their efforts to avoid the problem are adding unnecessary stress to an already stressful job. Add to that the typical worries that accompany any and every school day, and it's no wonder that teachers become burned out and stressed out under the burden of it all.

Stress robs you of the joy of living. Other people can often see that happening before you do. It's important to surround yourself with people who love you enough to tell you when the strain of life is showing on your face in ways that you cannot see.

You can't always feel the cumulative effect of a multitude of stressors, which is why it's also important to learn all you can about stress and anxiety—which often go hand in hand— and how to avoid the damage they can cause in your life. The place to start, as always, is with your Bible, especially the psalms. They not only provide comfort but also document the anxiety David and other writers experienced, as well as the relief from anxiety that drawing close to God resulted in.

I Will

Trust God on a deeper level.

         yes   *no*

Let go of the unnecessary things that add stress
to my life.

         yes   *no*

Learn a variety of techniques for dealing with the
inevitable stress of life.

         yes   *no*

Educate myself about the harmful effects of anxiety.

         yes   *no*

Stop worrying about things over which I have
no control.

         yes   *no*

Discover what it means to be anxious for nothing.

         yes   *no*

Know when it's time to seek counsel to overcome the
effects of stress on my life.

         yes   *no*

Things to Do

☐ *Begin the practice of meditating on a calming Scripture verse throughout the day, changing verses as needed.*

☐ *Read Kenneth H. Cooper's* Can Stress Heal? *to learn how to make stress work in your favor.*

☐ *Develop a strong network of relationships with people in your professional life and your personal life with whom you can safely unload your stress.*

☐ *Begin an exercise program, making sure you choose a stress-relieving activity—such as walking or swimming—that you enjoy.*

☐ *List the sources of anxiety in your life. Then read Matthew 6 meditatively; when you're done, cast all your anxiety—your list—on Jesus (1 Peter 5:7).*

Things to Remember

Cast all your anxiety on him, because he cares for you.

1 PETER 5:7 NRSV

Jesus said to His disciples, "Therefore I say to you, do not worry about your life, what you will eat; nor about the body, what you will put on."

LUKE 12:22 NKJV

Jesus said: "All these things the nations of the world seek after, and your Father knows that you need these things."

LUKE 12:30 NKJV

Jesus said, "Don't worry about the food or drink you need to live, or about the clothes you need for your body. Life is more than food, and the body is more than clothes."

MATTHEW 6:25 NCV

Jesus asked: "Which of you by worrying can add one cubit to his stature?"

MATTHEW 6:27 NKJV

Trust in the LORD, and do good; dwell in the land, and feed on His faithfulness.

PSALM 37:3 NKJV

We have a lot of anxieties, and one cancels out another very often.
—WINSTON CHURCHILL

God never built a Christian strong enough to carry today's duties and tomorrow's anxieties piled on the top of them.
—THEODORE L. CUYLER

Flexibility

Change for the Better

Paul wrote: "To those who are weak, I became weak so I could win the weak. I have become all things to all people so I could save some of them in any way possible."

—1 CORINTHIANS 9:22 NCV

It was late January, and Mrs. Jenkins was on a tight schedule to prepare her sixth-graders for mandatory statewide testing scheduled for mid-February. As she left school one Friday afternoon, she did so with a steely resolve to get back on track with her test preparation schedule the following Monday. But early Saturday morning, the unthinkable happened: The space shuttle Columbia broke up only minutes before its scheduled landing, killing all seven astronauts on board. It was February 1, 2003.

After the initial shock had passed, Mrs. Jenkins channeled the grief and horror she felt into panic over what she would do on Monday. She had exactly two weeks to cover two weeks' worth of test prep material. A poor showing on the test would not only reflect badly on her and her students but also would affect her entire school's "report-card" grade, issued yearly by the state education department. On Sunday, she spent a good deal of time in prayer about the situation and on the phone with several other teachers.

By Monday morning, Mrs. Jenkins was confident in her decision. Her students would be shaken up by the tragedy and hardly in a state of mind conducive to preparing for a standardized test. They had followed Columbia's mission in their science classes and had more than a passing interest in the project. As children, the deaths of the astronauts, and the visual images of the debris-strewn landscape would affect them deeply. On Monday *and* Tuesday, Mrs. Jenkins scrapped her test-oriented lesson plans and led the class in a discussion about the tragedy, the pros and cons of space travel, and the news coverage of the event. Toward the end of the second session, the students wrote about their feelings and reactions to the event.

Had Mrs. Jenkins stayed with her original plan, she would have missed out on a profound and significant teachable moment—and her students would have missed out on an opportunity to express their feelings and think about the accident within the safe confines of her classroom. Her flexibility did not go unrewarded; she was able to cover the test material easily in the remaining time, and her students' performance was exactly what she had hoped it would be.

Sometimes events will throw your schedule a curve. Remember this: Nothing comes as a surprise to God. He knows everything that is going to happen. When something comes along to upset your carefully laid-out plans, turn to God to discover the new direction He's pointing you in.

I Will

Be open to whatever God has in store for me. _____ yes _____ no

Realize that opinions change but biblical truth does not. _____ yes _____ no

Make allowances for different levels of maturity in my students and my colleagues. _____ yes _____ no

Realize that it's normal, but not always wise, to be resistant to change. _____ yes _____ no

Adapt my teaching style to accommodate the needs of my students. _____ yes _____ no

Be honest about areas of my life in which I am too rigid. _____ yes _____ no

Things to Do

☐ Select a teaching method or project that you are unhealthily attached to, and switch to something completely different.

☐ Start a list of the things you would most like to change about your classroom, your teaching style, and your lesson planning, and begin to implement some of those changes immediately.

☐ Rate your flexibility when it comes to varying your routine to meet the needs of a student who requires extra attention.

☐ Identify a recent proposed change in your district or school that you disagreed with, and with an open mind investigate its merits from the viewpoint of its advocates.

☐ Attend the next school board or education association meeting; noticing how often inflexibility hampers the group's ability to make decisions.

Things to Remember

Receive one who is weak in the faith, but not to disputes over doubtful things.

ROMANS 14:1 NKJV

You must make allowance for each other's faults and forgive the person who offends you. Remember, the Lord forgave you, so you must forgive others.

COLOSSIANS 3:13 NLT

One person esteems one day above another; another esteems every day alike. Let each be fully convinced in his own mind.

ROMANS 14:5 NKJV

God said: "Behold, I will do a new thing, now it shall spring forth; shall you not know it? I will even make a road in the wilderness and rivers in the desert."

ISAIAH 43:19 NKJV

Jesus told them this parable: "No one tears a patch from a new garment and sews it on an old one. If he does, he will have torn the new garment, and the patch from the new will not match the old."

LUKE 5:36 NIV

Jesus said: "I've come to change everything, turn everything rightside up—how I long for it to be finished!"

LUKE 12:50 THE MESSAGE

God grant me the serenity to accept the things I cannot change, the courage to change the things I can, and the wisdom to know the difference.

—REINHOLD NIEBUHR

Enjoying success requires the ability to adapt. Only by being open to change will you have a true opportunity to get the most from your talent.

—NOLAN RYAN

Creativity

Hidden Talent

---

*WHO HAS KNOWN THE MIND OF THE LORD, THAT HE WILL INSTRUCT HIM?
But we have the mind of Christ.*

—1 CORINTHIANS 2:16 NASB

Unless you teach art, music, graphic design, or any other subject categorized as a creative art, you may not consider yourself to be what is commonly considered "creative." But the ultimate Creator created you, and He gave you an imagination, along with the capacity for innovation, inspiration, originality, and other qualities associated with creativity.

Any time you have developed a new method for teaching your subject or solved a classroom problem in a unique way or customized a curriculum for the specific needs of *this* year's students instead of *last* year's students, you've used your God-given creativity. It doesn't matter what your subject area is or what grade level you teach; when you understand the broader meaning of creativity, you realize that a high-school calculus teacher can be just as creative as a kindergarten teacher.

Here are some real-life examples: A history teacher developed a game based on the TV show *Jeopardy* that was tailored to the curriculum her classes were using. Some schools celebrate Pi Day in math class each year on March 14 (3/14), in honor of *pi*, the number 3.14; the students use pizzas or other varieties of "pie" to demonstrate math problems using *pi*. Teachers in Minnesota created a "half-grade" promotion system that allows special education students to advance a half-grade instead of facing the stigma of being kept back a grade. In each case, the teachers used their creativity to stimulate student interest.

Teacher resources in print and on the Internet are loaded with creative ideas that you can incorporate into your classroom. But you already have the resources within yourself to come up with your own. You just need to believe that God has given you the ability to be creative, and then tap into the reservoir of creativity within you.

Christian artist Julia Cameron sees that reservoir as a well-stocked trout pond that needs to be maintained to avoid becoming depleted or stagnant. As you draw on your creative resources, you need to replenish the supply—or "restock the trout pond," as she puts it.

One way to do that is to frequently and intentionally open up to new ideas and new ways of looking at objects and situations. A simple way to do that is to learn a new skill, such as gourmet cooking or woodworking—any creative activity that involves working with your hands. Those are particularly good to start out with, because you can see and touch and hold the fruit of your labor.

Other creative prompts make use of your brain more than your hands. Most often, people associate creativity with giving free rein to their imagination, and so they think of the creative process in terms of big-picture thinking. But that's not always the case; sometimes, a bit of restriction can reap huge creative benefits. For example, try sitting still for what will seem like an exceedingly long time—say a half-hour—and simply observe one object, such as the bark on a tree or single flower. Or open the dictionary at random and place your finger on one entry; write down that word and think of as many associations with it that you can; the word *random*, for example, can remind you of random numbers, random acts of kindness, choosing something at random, even Random House publishers. A simple, free-association activity like that can help get your brain unstuck when it comes to the practical areas of your life.

Once you've tapped in to your own creativity, you're better able to encourage creativity in your students. Very young students generally need little prompting, but older ones are likely to have shut down their creative abilities out of fear of ridicule or memories of past rejection of their creativity. Both you and your students need to have the freedom to express your creative nature in an emotionally safe environment; you can find that for yourself, but you need to make sure you create that for your students.

There's no reason you should go through life denying yourself the opportunity to be creative. The Creator created you to be creative. Give yourself credit for the ways in which you are already using your creativity—and then launch out into new areas that will stretch your skills and talents.

I Will

Realize that God has created me to be creative.

yes _____ no _____

Encourage my students to develop their creativity.

yes _____ no _____

Recognize my God-given talent for innovation.

yes _____ no _____

Maintain a fresh perspective by trying new things.

yes _____ no _____

Believe that I have the mind of Christ.

yes _____ no _____

Remember that all creativity comes from God.

yes _____ no _____

Give others the freedom to think, live, and act
creatively, without judgment.

yes _____ no _____

Things to Do

☐ Memorize Psalm 139:13–16 and consider the creativity that went in to creating you.

☐ Inject a fresh dose of creativity into your teaching methods by reading a book like Spirit-Filled Teaching, by Ron Zuck.

☐ Ask several colleagues for the names of the top three Web sites they use to search for new ideas for their classrooms and their lessons, and visit those sites.

☐ Try at least one entirely new-to-you technique for teaching, such as a PowerPoint or multimedia presentation.

☐ Learn a creative skill that is completely alien to you, such as designing a Web site, writing poetry, or filmmaking.

☐ Devise a way to reward or acknowledge your students for creative thinking or action.

Things to Remember

Paul said, "In Him we live and move and have our being, as also some of your own poets have said, 'For we are also His offspring.' "

ACTS 17:28 NKJV

Then my God put the idea into my head that I should gather the nobles, leaders, and people so that they could check their genealogy. I found the book with the genealogy of those who came back the first time. I found the following written in it.

NEHEMIAH 7:5 GOD'S WORD

> *Each of you must take responsibility for doing the creative best you can with your own life.*
> Galatians 6:5 THE MESSAGE

Jesus said: "I want you to be smart in the same way—but for what is right—using every adversity to stimulate you to creative survival, to concentrate your attention on the bare essentials, so you'll live, really live, and not complacently just get by on good behavior."

LUKE 16:9 THE MESSAGE

I'll create praise on their lips: "Perfect peace to those both far and near." "I'll heal them," says the LORD.

ISAIAH 57:19 GOD'S WORD

The Lord said: "I will create a new heaven and a new earth. Past things will not be remembered. They will not come to mind."

ISAIAH 65:17 GOD'S WORD

We have different gifts, according to the grace given us.

ROMANS 12:6 NIV

Make a careful exploration of who you are and the work you have been given, and then sink yourself into that. Don't be impressed with yourself. Don't compare yourself with others.

GALATIANS 6:4 THE MESSAGE

God created man in His own image; in the image of God He created him; male and female He created them.

GENESIS 1:27 NKJV

We look at this Son and see the God who cannot be seen. We look at this Son and see God's original purpose in everything created.

COLOSSIANS 1:15 THE MESSAGE

We are His workmanship, created in Christ Jesus for good works, which God prepared beforehand that we should walk in them.

EPHESIANS 2:10 NKJV

If anyone is in Christ, he is a new creation; old things have passed away; behold, all things have become new.

2 CORINTHIANS 5:17 NKJV

Creativity involves breaking out of established patterns in order to look at things in a different way.

—EDWARD DE BONO

Make visible what, without you, might perhaps never have been seen.

—ROBERT BRESSON

Kindness

Benign Correction

As the elect of God, holy and beloved, put on tender mercies, kindness, humility, meekness, longsuffering.
—COLOSSIANS 3:12 NKJV

Kindness is all about showing your students that you care about them in a way that connects with their level of understanding. Everything you do in the classroom may stem from a deep concern for your students, but you also need to demonstrate that concern in tangible ways.

Caring teachers are the ones who go the extra mile by becoming involved in extracurricular activities and acknowledging their students' achievements even when those accomplishments are made outside their own classrooms. Some teachers occasionally forgo their need for a break from their students and have lunch with them. Students begin to see their teachers as real people who genuinely care about them and their lives. That kind of openness leads to a deeper level of trust on the part of the students toward their teachers.

Kindness in the classroom takes many forms. It includes smiling and greeting each student by name, making eye contact with students, listening carefully, and paying close attention to what each student says and does. It involves creating a safe and nurturing environment, resisting the temptation to raise your voice, maintaining a positive attitude, and injecting a healthy dose of self-deprecating humor into class time. Most of all it means never belittling, ridiculing, or negatively criticizing a student.

Closely related to kindness is compassion. In recent history, Mother Teresa exemplified a life of compassion. She would have been the first to tell you, though, that it was not because of any quality unique to her; she simply decided early on in her life that she would see Jesus in every person—in other words, the love God had for each person and the evidence of His activity in each person's life. The model she followed, of course, was Jesus Himself, whose life on earth essentially defined compassion.

Kindness and compassion have the power to transform another person's life. Think back to the teachers and other adults who had the most profound impact on your life. Most people will remember a teacher who spoke a kind word at just the right time or offered a positive, affirming word of encouragement when it was most needed. A single act of kindness will be remembered long after the school year ends.

You may not ever see the visible results of the care and concern you show for your students, but you can be assured that the impact of your acts of kindness and compassion will influence their lives far into the future.

I Will

Understand that the kindness of God can lead to repentance. yes _____   no _____

Commit random acts of kindness. yes _____   no _____

Learn the difference between being socially nice and genuinely kind. yes _____   no _____

See kindness as a distinctive characteristic of a Christian. yes _____   no _____

Recognize the transforming nature of kindness. yes _____   no _____

Be kind even when disciplining my students. yes _____   no _____

Realize the value of treating every person I meet with kindness and compassion. yes _____   no _____

Things to Do

☐ *Show the movie* Pay It Forward *during class and later discuss it, if appropriate, or watch it on your own.*

☐ *Visit www.actsofkindness.org for free resources on teaching kindness and demonstrating it in your classroom.*

☐ *Clearly communicate to your students your commitment to treating them kindly, your insistence that they treat each other kindly, and your intention to maintain an emotionally safe environment for them.*

☐ *Read and reflect on the story of the Good Samaritan in Luke 10:30–37, researching the hostility at that time toward Samaritans, if you have the time.*

☐ *Get your class involved in committing anonymous random acts of kindness on campus and in their neighborhoods.*

☐ *Send a thank-you note to someone who has treated you kindly.*

Things to Remember

Pure and undefiled religion before God and the Father is this: to visit orphans and widows in their trouble, and to keep oneself unspotted from the world.

JAMES 1:27 NKJV

When He saw the multitudes, He was moved with compassion for them, because they were weary and scattered, like sheep having no shepherd.

MATTHEW 9:36 NKJV

The fruit of the Spirit is love, joy, peace, longsuffering, kindness, goodness, faithfulness, gentleness, self-control. Against such there is no law.

GALATIANS 5:22–23 NKJV

Be kind to one another, tenderhearted, forgiving one another, even as God in Christ forgave you.

EPHESIANS 4:32 NKJV

Whoever has this world's goods, and sees his brother in need, and shuts up his heart from him, how does the love of God abide in him?

1 JOHN 3:17 NKJV

Pursue peace with all people, and holiness, without which no one will see the Lord.

HEBREWS 12:14 NKJV

Kindness is loving people more than they deserve.

—JOSEPH JOUBERT

Do all the good you can. By all the means you can. In all the ways you can. In all the places you can. At all the times you can. To all the people you can. As long as ever you can.

—JOHN WESLEY

Future Confidence

If we hope for what we do not yet have, we wait for it patiently.
—ROMANS 8:25 NIV

Throughout your life, you have had many things that you have hoped for—a certain toy when you were a child, the attention of the right person when you were a teenager, acceptance at your first-choice college, and the ideal position in your preferred school district upon graduation. Now, as a teacher, your life is filled with personal and professional hopes and dreams, from the comparatively minor ones such as, "I hope I can get away for a few weeks this summer" to the profoundly important ones such as, "I hope Greg recovers from that accident in the gym last week."

If you were to list your hopes right now—all of them, every one you can think of, both the possible and the impossible dreams—your list would likely be a long one. Even in this age of cynicism, most people can't help but hold out hope for the future, or at least for *their* future. They may not have much hope for world peace, but they can see a bigger house or a better car for themselves.

Those are all momentary, temporal hopes, even if they last for years—or a lifetime. Surpassing all of those individual hopes is *hope*—singular. That's a longing for purpose, for meaning, for some significance in life on earth and beyond. And that's the hope of the Incarnation—God coming to earth in the form of a man named Jesus whose death and resurrection holds the promise of an abundant life here on earth and eternal life with Him in heaven.

The psalms of David are filled with hope, even in the midst of unimaginable circumstances. Read some of his psalms and research a bit about his life. He seldom had much of a rest from his enemies, and even his own flesh and blood sought to kill him. Like any human being, he had his moments of despair. But many of his psalms show how quickly his dejected, lonely heart remembered to turn to God, because he had worked hope in its singular form into his present situation. "Why am I discouraged? Why so sad? I will put my hope in God!" he writes, almost as if he's wondering why he didn't think of that in the first place, before he sank into discouragement (Psalm 42:11 NLT). His ultimate hope in God, the hope that gave significance and meaning and purpose to his life, gave him the hope he needed in the ever-present danger he seemed to face.

That's how hope works in your life as well. Your abiding hope in God fuels your individual hopes for yourself, your loved ones, your colleagues, and your students. Think about that for a while: If your life did not rest on your hope in God, you would probably have few tangible reasons to continue hoping that one of your relatives would come to faith in God or that your colleague's marriage would be restored or that your most challenging student will ever see his high-school diploma. But with God, you know that all that and much more is possible. Your hope for the here and now rests on the hope you have in the eternal God.

The book of Hebrews calls hope an anchor for your soul. That's an appropriate metaphor, because an anchor keeps a ship from drifting along with the current, far from where it's supposed to be. Without the hope you have in God, your soul would likely be drifting along with the current of conventional wisdom—the wisdom of this world. Discouragement might get the better of you: There's no way my brother will ever come to faith in Christ; my friend just ought to divorce that guy she's married to; Kyle is just taking up valuable space and time and effort in my classroom—there's no way that kid will ever graduate.

Keep the hope you have in God constantly in front of you. When your hope begins to falter—and it will—hold on tightly to your plural hopes for the here and now as well as that singular hope that rests in your eternal future in God's presence. Your hope is a living hope founded on the resurrection of the living Jesus. It's a hope that will never fail you.

I Will

Place my hope in God.   _yes_ _no_

Maintain a hopeful attitude toward the future.   _yes_ _no_

Model hopefulness for my students and colleagues.   _yes_ _no_

Remember that my ultimate hope is heaven.   _yes_ _no_

Meditate on the promises of God.   _yes_ _no_

Visualize my future from God's perspective.   _yes_ _no_

Replace my worry with hope.   _yes_ _no_

Things to Do

☐ Take one of your greatest hopes for your future on earth and pray about it to determine if it is God's will for your life.

☐ Write out a prayer that expresses the hope you have in God.

☐ Identify some specific hopes that you have for your students—such as success, strong character, relationship with God—and write them down to remind yourself of your purpose in their lives.

☐ Use a concordance to find all the references to hope in either Psalms or Romans, and memorize the ones that most resonate with you.

☐ Share the thoughts expressed in the quotes on the following pages with someone who has lost hope.

☐ List some ways you can impart a sense of hope to your students.

☐ Look up hope in a dictionary and compare its definition with your understanding of hope from a biblical perspective.

Things to Remember

David wrote: "I have set the Lord continually before me; because He is at my right hand, I shall not be moved. Therefore my heart is glad and my glory [my inner self] rejoices; my body too shall rest and confidently dwell in safety."

PSALM 16:8–9 AMP

David wrote: "Why am I discouraged? Why so sad? I will put my hope in God! I will praise him again—my Savior and my God!"

PSALM 42:11 NLT

We also rejoice in our sufferings, because we know that suffering produces perseverance; perseverance, character; and character, hope.

Romans 5:3–4 NIV

This hope we have as an anchor of the soul, both sure and steadfast, and which enters the Presence behind the veil.

HEBREWS 6:19 NKJV

Blessed be the God and Father of our Lord Jesus Christ, who according to His abundant mercy has begotten us again to a living hope through the resurrection of Jesus Christ from the dead.

1 PETER 1:3 NKJV

I depend on you, and I have trusted you since I was young.

PSALM 71:5 CEV

Christ is pure, and all who have this hope in Christ keep themselves pure like Christ.

1 JOHN 3:3 NCV

Take my side as you promised; I'll live then for sure. Don't disappoint all my grand hopes.

PSALM 119:116 THE MESSAGE

Paul wrote: "Now may our Lord Jesus Christ Himself, and our God and Father, who has loved us and given us everlasting consolation and good hope by grace, comfort your hearts and establish you in every good word and work."

2 THESSALONIANS 2:16–17 NKJV

I'm glad from the inside out—ecstatic; I've pitched my tent in the land of hope.

ACTS 2:26 THE MESSAGE

There is surely a future hope for you, and your hope will not be cut off.

PROVERBS 23:18 NIV

David wrote: "Lord, you are my shield, my glory, and my only hope. You alone can lift my head, now bowed in shame."

PSALM 3:3 TLB

Hope . . . is not the conviction that something will turn out well, but the certainty that something makes sense, regardless of how it turns out.
—VACLAV HAVEL

We must accept finite disappointment, but never lose infinite hope.
—MARTIN LUTHER KING JR.

Listening

Ears That Hear

Jesus said to them, "He who has ears to hear, let him hear!"

—MARK 4:9 NKJV

Chuck Swindoll, chancellor of Dallas Theological Seminary, tells of a time when he had allowed the "busyness" and demands of his life to interfere with his relationship with his wife and children. All of their interaction was rushed, to the point where he was treating them rudely. After yet another rushed meal one night, his young daughter blurted out that she had something important to tell him and she'd do it really fast.

Ashamed at her unintentional rebuke, Swindoll assured her that she didn't have to rush—she could talk to him slowly. "Then listen slowly," she replied.

That's good advice for everyone. Listening slowly shows the other person in a conversation that you are genuinely listening, not rushing to get through the conversation, not hurrying to get in your next response, not thinking of something else entirely. Intentional listening, in fact, has been called the highest compliment you can pay to another person, especially in the hurried pace of twenty-first-century life.

Most people can probably recall a time when a teacher listened too quickly and missed what the student was really saying. Likewise, though, many people have treasured memories of a teacher who took the time to listen slowly, who listened with his heart as well as his ears. Those are the teachers whose attentiveness says to the student, "I value who you are and what you have to say."

Developing the ability to listen slowly is both a horizontal activity, directed toward your students and everyone else in your life, and a vertical activity, directed toward God. Your attentiveness to God—your ability and willingness to hear Him speak to you through the Bible, through prayer, through people, and through circumstances—says to Him, "I value who you are, God, and what you have to say to me about my life."

Listening is a skill that can be learned, which means it is also a skill that can be taught. As you learn to become a better listener, to slow down and listen intentionally and purpose-fully to what God or another person has to say, you can pass those skills along to your students, by example and by specific instruction. And as you learn to listen with your ears to what is said, and with your heart to what is left unspoken, you'll be paying the people in your life the highest compliment ever, the gift of your undivided attention.

I Will

Practice being a careful listener.	_yes_	_no_
Learn to hear the voice of God.	_yes_	_no_
Listen with my heart as well as my ears.	_yes_	_no_
Give God my full attention when I pray or meditate.	_yes_	_no_
Realize that my students feel valued when I listen to them.	_yes_	_no_
Recognize the way God speaks to me.	_yes_	_no_
Understand that hearing God requires obeying Him as well.	_yes_	_no_

Things to Do

☐ *Get together with a colleague or two to talk about practical steps you can take to help your students become better listeners.*

☐ *Read John 10:27 and think about how you first realized you were hearing God calling you.*

☐ *Enter "hearing God's voice" into a search engine on a Christian site and read several of the resulting files (they're usually devotionals).*

☐ *Go through the day tomorrow taking note of how often your mind starts to wander when someone else is talking—and how others seem to have the same problem when you are talking.*

☐ *Give your students specific verbal directions on a task they are to perform and see how many follow your instructions correctly; use the results as an example of the need for good listening skills.*

Things to Remember

Jesus said: "My sheep hear My voice, and I know them, and they follow Me."

JOHN 10:27 NKJV

So then, my beloved brethren, let every man be swift to hear, slow to speak, slow to wrath.

JAMES 1:19 NKJV

This is what the LORD says—your Redeemer, the Holy One of Israel: "I am the LORD your God, who teaches you what is best for you, who directs you in the way you should go."

ISAIAH 48:17 NIV

One who looks intently at the perfect law, the law of liberty, and abides by it, not having become a forgetful hearer but an effectual doer, this man will be blessed in what he does.

JAMES 1:25 NASB

Jesus said: "The gatekeeper opens the gate for him, and the sheep hear his voice and come to him. He calls his own sheep by name and leads them out."

JOHN 10:3 NLT

If you have ears, then, listen to what the Spirit says to the churches!

REVELATION 2:29 GNT

A good listener is not only popular everywhere, but after a while he knows something.

—WILSON MIZNER

The greatest gift you can give another is the purity of your attention.

—RICHARD MOSS

Purpose

Head Start

---

*"I know the plans I have for you," declares the Lᴏʀᴅ,
"plans to prosper you and not to harm you, plans to give
you hope and a future."*

—Jᴇʀᴇᴍɪᴀʜ 29:11 ɴɪᴠ

Every Wednesday, Pauline Hord drove a hundred miles each way to a prison to teach inmates how to read and write so they could become functioning, productive members of society upon their release. Most of the rest of the week she spent in public schools, training teachers in a new literacy method. Her tireless efforts on behalf of the thousands of illiterate people in the Memphis area brought her to the attention of President George H. Bush, who had earlier launched his "Points of Light" program to recognize people who exercised a positive influence on their communities.

On a trip through Memphis some time later, President Bush invited the city's seven "Points of Light" to have lunch with him. But the president of the United States failed to run his plans by Pauline first. He scheduled the luncheon for a Wednesday, the day the prisoners would be expecting her visit. She declined the president's invitation, and there was one "Point of Light" missing from the luncheon that day.

Pauline Hord's purpose clearly drove her life. But her purpose had value beyond the here and now. As a Christian, she was committed to sharing the love of God with the prisoners. Her passion for teaching them to read was rooted in her hope and prayer that they would one day be able to read the Bible for themselves. Not even lunch with the president could distract her from the overarching purpose of her life.

Rick Warren, pastor of Saddleback Church in Orange County, California, believes every Christian has been planned for God's pleasure, formed to be part of God's family, created to become like Christ, shaped for God's service, and made to tell others about Christ. Like Pauline Hord, teaching may be one of the unique purposes for your life, but God also has a larger purpose, one that encompasses the five areas Warren identified. By coupling your unique purpose with God's primary purpose, your influence on the lives of others can be immeasurable.

Even if you're not clear on what your individual purpose in life is, make sure you have a solid understanding that God's purpose for you is a combination of *worship, fellowship, discipleship, ministry,* and *mission*—the five words that correspond with Warren's descriptions. With those elements in place, your life will be driven by an unchanging purpose that carries you from one job to another—even one career to another—and keeps your focus steady and sure on the things that matter most, things of eternal consequence.

I Will

Believe that there is a purpose for my life beyond what I can see.

yes _no_

Realize that one of my main purposes in life is to love and worship God.

yes _no_

Trust God to reveal the specific plans He has for me.

yes _no_

Understand that my goals need to be shaped in cooperation with God.

yes _no_

Minister to those whose lives seem to lack purpose.

yes _no_

Help my students to realize that their lives have meaning and purpose.

yes _no_

Be thankful that my everyday life is not all there is.

yes _no_

Things to Do

☐ Read The Purpose Driven Life, by Rick Warren, or join a "40 Days of Purpose" study group.

☐ Write down every reason you can think of that you are on earth right now. Pray over the list, asking God to show you the things you missed.

☐ Discover what your spiritual gifts are, using any one of the many resources available online.

☐ List the five purposes identified by Warren and next to each one identify the ways in which your life exemplifies the corresponding purpose.

☐ Determine what action steps you need to take to better align your life with God's purposes—such as finding a way to serve in your church or enrolling in a discipleship class.

Things to Remember

Paul wrote: "Make my joy complete by being like-minded, having the same love, being one in spirit and purpose."

PHILIPPIANS 2:2 NIV

Many plans are in a man's mind, but it is the Lord's purpose for him that will stand.

PROVERBS 19:21 AMP

Don't get ahead of the Master and jump to conclusions with your judgments before all the evidence is in. When he comes, he will bring out in the open and place in evidence all kinds of things we never even dreamed of—inner motives and purposes and prayers. Only then will any one of us get to hear the "Well done!" of God.

1 CORINTHIANS 4:5 THE MESSAGE

And it shall come to pass afterward that I will pour out My Spirit on all flesh; your sons and your daughters shall prophesy, your old men shall dream dreams, your young men shall see visions.

JOEL 2:28 NKJV

For God is at work within you, helping you want to obey him, and then helping you do what he wants.

PHILIPPIANS 2:13 TLB

Above all be of single aim; have a legitimate and useful purpose, and devote yourself unreservedly to it.

—JAMES ALLEN

The only true happiness comes from squandering ourselves for a purpose.

—JOHN MASON BROWN

Forgiveness

Letting It Go

Be gentle and ready to forgive; never hold grudges. Remember,
the Lord forgave you, so you must forgive others.

—COLOSSIANS 3:13 TLB

Throughout the school year, Mrs. Harrison had held her
tongue every time Mr. Dubois made a sarcastic, cutting remark
to other teachers—including her. More than one teacher had
lost their temper with him, but he simply shrugged off their
complaints by accusing them of not having any semblance of a
sense of humor. What made the situation worse was that
Mr. Dubois was a high-profile Christian in the community,
frequently in the news for spearheading short-term mission
trips to Guatemala, recruiting volunteers to work with him in
his church's soup kitchen, and serving as a lay chaplain at the
local hospital.

One afternoon, the perfect opportunity arose to talk to
him about the way he treated other people and the poor
reflection his behavior was on Christ. She and Mr. Dubois were
the only two teachers in the faculty lounge at the time, and she
knew she had to speak up. Phrasing her comments as tactfully
and graciously as she knew how, she emphasized that she
knew he was just kidding around, suggesting that perhaps he

did not realize how his remarks came across to others. Mr. Dubois looked at her intently and thoughtfully the whole time she spoke, nodding in agreement. When she finished, he opened his mouth as if to speak—and burst into laughter. "You've got to be kidding me! You're telling me how to act? I don't think so," he said. At that moment, another teacher entered the room, and Mr. Dubois began recounting—as dramatically as possible—what Mrs. Harrison had just said to him. Humiliated, she left the room, part of her feeling hurt but most of her feeling vengeful.

What she did not know was that Miss Scott, the teacher who had to listen to Mr. Dubois's tirade, fully supported Mrs. Harrison and her rightfulness in confronting him about his sarcasm. He had hurt and angered a lot of people, she said, and many teachers were avoiding the faculty lounge for that very reason. It was time he knew, and she was glad her colleague had spoken up.

When classes resumed after spring break several weeks later, Mr. Dubois found Mrs. Harrison alone in her classroom. Clearly repentant, he acknowledged his ongoing inappropriate behavior as well as his rudeness and unkind treatment of her when she had tried to reason with him. "There was so much talk about forgiveness at church over Easter that I couldn't help but hear what God was saying to me," he said. "I was wrong, and I've been wrong for a long time. Will you forgive me?"

Mrs. Harrison hesitated. She momentarily wondered if this was another one of his ruses. Would he burst out laughing in ridicule if she extended forgiveness? But she knew what she had to do: Regardless of his response, her responsibility as a follower of Christ was to make the decision to forgive him and extend that forgiveness out loud. "I forgive you," she said. Mr. Dubois thanked her—and asked her to hold him accountable for his words. "Don't wait till I've crossed the line," he said. "I want you to tell me right away, even if I've moved just an inch closer to the line." With that, he left the room, resolved to close out the school year on a more positive note.

Forgiveness, both seeking it and extending it, is a powerful force in transforming a person's life. The greatest transformation, of course, comes when you ask God's forgiveness, accept it, and begin to live out your life as a new creation (2 Corinthians 5:17). It's also transforming when you realize you have wronged another person and seek his forgiveness. He may forgive you—or he may not. The only aspect of that interaction that you have any control over is your own, and you've done what you could by asking for forgiveness (and making restitution, if appropriate). If he refuses to forgive you, you need to move on and not dwell on his response.

Forgiveness works both ways. Just as you would like others to forgive you, they would like you to forgive them. By remembering how freely and how readily God forgave you, you should seldom have a problem forgiving someone else. And that includes yourself, possibly the hardest person for you to forgive.

I Will

Believe that forgiveness has the power to transform a person's life.

_____ yes   _____ no

Realize that extending forgiveness is as important as seeking it.

_____ yes   _____ no

Be thankful for God's forgiveness.

_____ yes   _____ no

Remember to forgive myself.

_____ yes   _____ no

Recognize forgiveness as a decision of the will.

_____ yes   _____ no

Never forget how freely I have been forgiven.

_____ yes   _____ no

Things to Do

☐ *Ask God to show you if there is someone you have wronged and need to seek their forgiveness.*

☐ *Read the accounts of forgiveness on the part of victims' parents in school tragedies such as Columbine and Paducah (use a search engine to find relevant stories).*

☐ *Pray the Lord's Prayer (Matthew 6:9–13), replacing the plural pronouns with singular pronouns to make it more personal—"My Father, who art in heaven . . ."*

☐ *Research the negative health effects of a lack of forgiveness.*

☐ *Ask God to reveal to you the names of people you may need to forgive; intentionally forgive them, in their presence, if possible, and in your heart.*

☐ *Read Matthew 18:21–35 (the parable of the unmerciful servant) for its lesson on forgiveness.*

Things to Remember

Jesus said: "In prayer there is a connection between what God does and what you do. You can't get forgiveness from God, for instance, without also forgiving others."

MATTHEW 6:14 THE MESSAGE

While council members were executing Stephen, he called out, "Lord Jesus, welcome my spirit." Then he knelt down and shouted, "Lord, don't hold this sin against them." After he had said this, he died.

ACTS 7:59–60 GOD'S WORD

Then Jesus said, "Father, forgive them, for they do not know what they do." And they divided His garments and cast lots.

Luke 23:34 NKJV

Then Peter came to Him and said, "Lord, how often shall my brother sin against me, and I forgive him? Up to seven times?" Jesus said to him, "I do not say to you, up to seven times, but up to seventy times seven."

MATTHEW 18:21–22 NKJV

Beloved, do not avenge yourselves, but rather give place to wrath; for it is written, "Vengeance is Mine, I will repay," says the Lord.

ROMANS 12:19 NKJV

In Christ we are set free by the blood of his death, and so we have forgiveness of sins. How rich is God's grace, which he has given to us so fully and freely. God, with full wisdom and understanding, let us know his secret purpose. This was what God wanted, and he planned to do it through Christ.

EPHESIANS 1:7–9 NCV

Jesus said, "I assure you that any sin can be forgiven."

MARK 3:28 NLT

Jesus said, "And forgive us our sins, for we also forgive everyone who is indebted to us."

LUKE 11:4 NKJV

The LORD said: "The past troubles will be forgotten and hidden from my eyes."

ISAIAH 65:16 NIV

Jesus said, "When you are praying, first forgive anyone you are holding a grudge against, so that your Father in heaven will forgive your sins, too."

MARK 11:25 NLT

If we confess our sins, He is faithful and righteous to forgive us our sins and to cleanse us from all unrighteousness.

1 JOHN 1:9 NASB

"I can forgive, but I cannot forget," is only another way of saying, "I cannot forgive."

—HENRY WARD BEECHER

There is no revenge so complete as forgiveness.

—JOSH BILLINGS

Friendliness

Pleasant and Pleasing

Tell them [fellow believers] not to speak evil of anyone, but to be peaceful and friendly, and always to show a gentle attitude toward everyone.

—TITUS 3:2 GNT

Mrs. Haskins remembered it well—a day toward the beginning of her teaching career when she was representing her school district at a national education conference. She was the sole teacher from her region, and it seemed everyone else there knew at least two or three other people. The chumminess of the others in attendance intensified her loneliness and lack of confidence. Though she had tried hard to focus on the presentations made by the many talented educators at the sessions she attended, a part of her couldn't wait until the conference was over.

As she stood in the lunch buffet line on the second day, she felt a tap on her shoulder. Another registrant invited Mrs. Haskins to join her and two other teachers at their table for four. Grateful, she accepted. Only later did she discover that the three had realized several hours earlier that she appeared to be completely alone, and they decided as a group to take advantage of their first opportunity to extend a welcome to her.

You have probably been on the receiving end of a similar friendly gesture at some point in your life, as well as on the giving end. If so, you know the difference it can make in a person's day or, like Mrs. Haskins, in their memories of a particular event in their lives. It takes so little, really, to make a huge impact on another person, simply by being pleasant, extending an informal invitation to join in a conversation, treating the person with kindness and courtesy, or making a friendly overture of some kind.

As a Christian, the friendliness you offer to those around you speaks volumes about your relationship with God. Jesus addressed this in the Sermon on the Mount. "If you are nice only to your friends, you are no better than other people," He said to the crowd who had come to hear Him speak. "Even those who don't know God are nice to their friends" (Matthew 5:47 NCV). Your "niceness"—your friendliness—is only as valuable as the extent of its reach. If you are pleasant only to your friends, that value is severely limited.

Make it a habit to maintain a friendly attitude toward others. It's one of the easiest habits you can acquire. Ask God to keep reminding you that you can make a difference to other people simply by smiling at them, welcoming them, being helpful—acknowledging their importance to you and to God.

I Will

Recognize the value of having a friendly attitude toward everyone.

yes *no*

Be pleasant to others even if they never return the same courtesy.

yes *no*

Take the initiative in reaching out to others.

yes *no*

Appreciate the uniqueness of each individual.

yes *no*

See encounters with other people as God-ordained opportunities for ministry.

yes *no*

Make others feel welcome in my presence and in my home.

yes *no*

Things to Do

☐ *Come up with ideas for practicing hospitality with your colleagues, such as putting out snacks for everyone in the teachers' lounge or helping to plan a faculty get-together.*

☐ *Make a point of speaking to faculty or staff members you may have unintentionally overlooked in the past.*

☐ *Invite colleagues to your home for a short-term reading group, Bible study, or discussion group on a spiritual topic.*

☐ *Take extra care in the way you interact with salespeople, food servers, and clerks over the next few days and notice the difference it makes in their demeanor.*

☐ *Surprise someone on the support staff at your school with a friendly gesture, such as a birthday card, small gift, or thoughtful note.*

☐ *On your own or with another teacher, define the boundaries of friendly behavior toward your students.*

Things to Remember

[Christians] spent their time in learning from the apostles, taking part in the fellowship, and sharing in the fellowship meals and the prayers.

ACTS 2:42 GNT

John wrote to the Christian congregations: "We announce to you what we have seen and heard, because we want you also to have fellowship with us. Our fellowship is with God the Father and with his Son, Jesus Christ."

1 JOHN 1:3 NCV

We [David and his friends] had intimate talks with each other and worshiped together in the Temple.

PSALM 55:14 GNT

Those who had respect for the LORD talked with one another. They cheered each other up. And the LORD heard them. A list of people and what they did was written on a scroll in front of him. It included the names of those who respected the LORD and honored him.

MALACHI 3:16 NIrV

If we walk in the light as He is in the light, we have fellowship with one another, and the blood of Jesus Christ His Son cleanses us from all sin.

1 JOHN 1:7 NKJV

A good motto is: Use friendliness but do not use your friends.

—FRANK CRANE

Lead the life that will make you kind and friendly to everyone about you, and you will be surprised what a happy life you will lead.

—CHARLES M. SCHWAB

Higher Education

Oh, the depth of the riches both of the wisdom and knowledge of God! How unsearchable are His judgments and His ways past finding out!

—ROMANS 11:33 NKJV

Some time after becoming a *sadhu*—a Hindu ascetic—a young man named Sundar Singh became despondent to the point of wanting to take his own life. The night before he planned to carry out the act, he prayed one last time and asked God to reveal Himself. He did. But Singh was not expecting the God that was revealed, the God of Christianity. So compelling was his experience that night that Singh renounced Hinduism and embraced a passionate belief in Jesus Christ, leading his family to reject and even attempt to poison him.

Singh eventually went to seminary for training, but throughout his life it was his devotion to prayer, meditation, Bible reading, service to others, and living in the presence of God that drew him closer to God and molded him into one of India's most influential indigenous evangelists. His life was saved and transformed all because of a simple prayer in which he asked God to make Himself known.

There's a lesson in Singh's story for those who are inclined to complicate what to God is a very simple matter. In many other faiths, the pathway to their deity is a long and complex one that involves an inordinate amount of effort on the part of a person seeking spiritual enlightenment. But the God of the Bible simply invites you to draw near to Him. If you would like to know who He is, He encourages you to ask Him who He is. If you would like to know Him better, He encourages you to spend time with Him. He even made sure that those who knew Him in the past left a record—the Bible—so you could discover the truth about Him.

The way you get to know God is in some respects the same way you get to know anyone. You spend time with the person, talking, asking questions, listening, enjoying his company, and, in this case, reading the sixty-six books His Spirit wrote to make sure you would never forget who He is and how much He loves you.

Singh's entire adult life was devoted to knowing God. Everything he did was directed toward that purpose, to the point that many people considered him eccentric. But few could argue with the fruit of that effort—a life that many say radiated the very presence of God. That kind of intimacy with God is available to everyone. All you have to do is to keep seeking God, and He'll take it from there.

I Will

Draw closer to God.

yes _____   _no_ _____

Recognize the many ways (Scripture, prayer, meditation, experience) that I can learn more about God and His ways.

yes _____   _no_ _____

Realize that God wants me to know Him better.

yes _____   _no_ _____

Accept the fact that I cannot know God fully.

yes _____   _no_ _____

Understand that getting to know God is a lifelong endeavor.

yes _____   _no_ _____

Pray that God's Spirit will reveal spiritual truth to me.

yes _____   _no_ _____

Be aware of God's activity in my life.

yes _____   _no_ _____

Things to Do

☐ *Read a book about who God is, such as* In the Face of God, *by Michael Horton;* Who Is God?, *by J. Vernon McGee; or the devotional* In the Presence of God, *by R. C. Sproul.*

☐ *Pray Psalm 34 back to God.*

☐ *Schedule at least a half-day, if possible, to get away by yourself to spend time in the presence of God.*

☐ *Do a Bible study on the attributes of God, using an online concordance such as* Nave's Topical Bible *at www.crosswalk.com.*

☐ *List the various ways you can get to know God and incorporate them into your regular devotional routine.*

☐ *Ask a teacher of another faith to talk about his or her belief about God and compare it with your understanding of the God of the Bible.*

Things to Remember

This is why you are great, Lord God! There is no one like you. There is no God except you. We have heard all this ourselves!

2 SAMUEL 7:22 NCV

No one has ever seen God. But his only Son, who is himself God, is near to the Father's heart; he has told us about him.

JOHN 1:18 NLT

Balaam said: "God is not a man, that He should lie, nor a son of man, that He should repent. Has He said, and will He not do? Or has He spoken, and will He not make it good?"

NUMBERS 23:19 NKJV

Glory in His holy name; let the hearts of those rejoice who seek the LORD! Seek the LORD and His strength; seek His face evermore!

1 CHRONICLES 16:10–11 NKJV

Oh, taste and see that the LORD is good; blessed is the man who trusts in Him! Oh, fear the LORD, you His saints! There is no want to those who fear Him.

PSALM 34:8–9 NKJV

Be still, and know that I am God; I will be exalted among the nations, I will be exalted in the earth!

PSALM 46:10 NKJV

People see God every day; they just don't recognize Him.

—PEARL BAILEY

A god who let us prove his existence would be an idol.

—DIETRICH BONHOEFFER

Values

Core Curriculum

Jesus said: "Where your treasure is, there your heart will be also."

—LUKE 12:34 NKJV

Math teacher Jerry Harrington tells of a time when a former student brought him up short in his daily, fifteen-minute "How to Be Successful" class at San Marcos Junior High School in Southern California. The student—one who hardly seemed interested in the course at the time—credited the course with giving him the incentive to get a job during high school to develop the necessary skills, and save some money, so he could escape the welfare-dependent fate of so many kids in his neighborhood. Harrington never would have guessed that the course had impacted this particular student to that extent, and his commitment to continue teaching the course became even stronger.

While the course offers a great deal of practical guidance such as action steps to take in getting your first job, at the heart of the curriculum are underlying lessons in establishing a positive value system for your life. The model program is especially appealing to Christian teachers who want to incorporate character and values education into their public school lessons but cannot use a Bible-based curriculum. As

Harrington and other teachers have discovered, exposing students to positive values using an intentional, focused curriculum teaches them not only the right way to live but also the reasons why that way is right. And while the debate continues over whether character education has a rightful place in public school classrooms, many teachers have discovered the sad fact that positive values are not being taught in the home, and children are often morally handicapped as a result.

Even if you are not able to offer a separate course on character education, you can begin to clarify for your students the values you consider essential to success in *life*—in becoming a person of high moral character. That means you need to have clearly defined values that guide your own life, as well as an understanding of the way they contribute to your success as a human being. Harrington's course defines its twelve core values in a series of "Be . . ." statements, such as "Be on time" and "Be polite," which help the students remember them better. You may want to do the same for yourself and especially when attempting to teach values in class.

But no matter how thorough a character education curriculum is, no matter how focused and how practical it is, nothing beats the power of a good example. By consistently modeling positive values in and out of your classroom, you are offering your students a lesson in right living that a character curriculum can enhance but not replace. When you live and work in a way consistent with your value structure, one that draws on the timeless wisdom of Scripture, your life becomes inseparable from your values. As author and management expert Joe Batten expresses it, "Our value is the sum of our values."

While instruction on the right way to live permeates the entire Bible, there are several sections that provide a concentrated education in positive values: the Sermon on the Mount, for one, and the entire book of Proverbs, for another. Paul's letters to Timothy can also be helpful in clarifying your value system, as can most of the psalms. In addition, numerous Christian books and other resources are available to assist you in identifying the values that should guide your life.

As many people have discovered, defining your values is the easy part; living in a way consistent with them presents a greater challenge. Take just one example, your commitment to placing a high value on honesty. You think you have that one down pat, but then you come up against the story of Rahab in Joshua 2, in which she hides two spies sent out by Joshua, lies to their pursuers about their whereabouts, and is blessed by God. That story could teach you the value of spiritual discernment—or give you an excuse to justify a lie you're tempted to tell. The Rahab story challenges believers to determine whether their value system would permit them to cross the line she crossed.

In all things, your highest priority must be your relationship with God and living in a way that pleases and glorifies Him. When you do that, you needn't be overly concerned about the example you're setting—your value system will become a natural outgrowth of that relationship.

I Will

Define my core values.

yes   _no_

Search the Scriptures for references to positive values.

yes   _no_

Make sure my values line up with biblical values.

yes   _no_

Realize that I am already an example to others of the values I live by.

yes   _no_

Live in a way that is pleasing to God.

yes   _no_

Recognize my responsibility in passing along positive values to my students.

yes   _no_

Things to Do

☐ *List your core values, including universal, biblical values like honesty and integrity, and others that are more personal, such as simplicity.*

☐ *Make a second list of the things you love and love to do; compare the two lists to see if there are discrepancies between your stated values and your lived values.*

☐ *Define several values that you would like to instill in your students and create a brief lesson on each one.*

☐ *Meditatively read the Sermon on the Mount, slowly allowing its truths to sink into your spirit.*

☐ *Search the Web for values-based curriculum programs appropriate for the grade level you teach.*

☐ *Read several articles that discuss both sides of the debate over character education in public schools and prepare a defense of your position on the issue.*

Things to Remember

Yet the righteous will hold to his way, and he who has clean hands will be stronger and stronger.

JOB 17:9 NKJV

Lead me, O LORD, in Your righteousness because of my enemies; make Your way straight before my face.

PSALM 5:8 NKJV

You will understand what is right and just and fair—every good path.
Proverbs 2:9 NIV

You, O LORD, will bless the righteous; with favor You will surround him as with a shield.

PSALM 5:12 NKJV

You who love the LORD, hate evil! He preserves the souls of His saints; He delivers them out of the hand of the wicked. Light is sown for the righteous, and gladness for the upright in heart. Rejoice in the LORD, you righteous, and give thanks at the remembrance of His holy name.

PSALM 97:10–12 NKJV

Keep your tongue from evil, and your lips from speaking deceit. Depart from evil and do good; seek peace and pursue it. The eyes of the LORD are on the righteous, and His ears are open to their cry.

PSALM 34:13–15 NKJV

The steps of a good man are ordered by the LORD, and He delights in his way. Though he fall, he shall not be utterly cast down; for the LORD upholds him with His hand.

PSALM 37:23–24 NKJV

Cast your burden on the LORD, and He shall sustain you; He shall never permit the righteous to be moved.

PSALM 55:22 NKJV

Men will say, "Surely there is a reward for the righteous; surely He is God who judges in the earth."

PSALM 58:11 NKJV

The humble He guides in justice, and the humble He teaches His way.

PSALM 25:9 NKJV

David shepherded them with integrity.

PSALM 78:72 NIV

Evil men do not seek justice, but those who seek the LORD understand all.

PROVERBS 28:5 NKJV

> Life's ups and downs provide windows of opportunity to determine your values and goals.
> —MARSHA SINETAR

> It is easier to exemplify values than teach them.
> —THEODORE M. HESBURGH

Tact

Diplomatic Dialogue

Now then, we are ambassadors for Christ, as though God were pleading through us: we implore you on Christ's behalf, be reconciled to God.

—2 CORINTHIANS 5:20 NKJV

The apostle Paul had a delicate situation to deal with. While in prison in Rome he became acquainted with a runaway slave named Onesimus, who became a Christian through Paul's influence. Onesimus rightfully belonged to a man named Philemon, who also had come to Christ under Paul's teaching and now hosted the Colossian church in his home.

Paul knew he had to return Onesimus to Philemon, but he had no control over the kind of treatment the slave would receive. His appeal to Philemon to receive Onesimus graciously and as a brother in Christ is a masterpiece in tactful communication. It's worth reading and studying, especially at a time when you need to handle an especially awkward or thorny situation.

Diplomats instinctively understand the need for careful, tactful communication. As ambassadors for their nations, they realize that a thoughtless comment or an insensitive handling of a situation may not only reflect badly on the nation they represent but also result in disastrous consequences. In describing himself as an ambassador for Christ in Philemon 1:9, Paul makes it clear that he is acting on behalf of Christ. And in reminding Christians that they, too, are ambassadors of Christ in his letter to the church at Corinth, Paul admonishes believers to always treat others with sensitivity and discretion.

Even if you work in a public school—in fact, especially if you work in a public school—you are Christ's ambassador to that campus. As His representative, your responsibility is to accurately reflect who He is by carefully communicating His teaching to others when possible, always treating people graciously and politely, and faithfully carrying out Christ's instructions—just like a diplomat. In every situation, you are to stand with Him, never compromising, never backing down from what He has called you to do, and you are to accomplish all that with unfailing courtesy.

That's a fairly heady assignment. The best diplomats make it look easy, though, because living by diplomatic principles has become second nature to them. That's the way it should be for Christians as well. Living in continual awareness that you are a representative of Christ will go a long way toward transforming you into a kinder, gentler, more tactful person, because you will naturally begin to respond to others as Christ would. Accept your role as an ambassador for Christ joyfully and expectantly, knowing that God will not leave you power-less to carry out the functions that come with the privilege of representing Him wherever you go.

I Will

	yes	no
Realize that I am an ambassador for Christ.	_yes_	_no_
Understand how hurtful tactlessness can be.	_yes_	_no_
Ask God's forgiveness for tactless remarks I've made.	_yes_	_no_
Recognize the need for diplomacy, especially in resolving disputes and in sharing my faith.	_yes_	_no_
Ask God to place His seal on my lips.	_yes_	_no_
Forgive those whose tactlessness has hurt me.	_yes_	_no_
Learn to think carefully before I speak.	_yes_	_no_

Things to Do

☐ *Read about the effect of Daniel's tactfulness in Daniel 2.*

☐ *Evaluate your daily routine in light of your understanding of what it means to be an ambassador of Christ.*

☐ *Recall a situation in which you responded tactlessly, and determine how you could have made your point more tactfully.*

☐ *Read the book of Philemon for a lesson in diplomacy.*

☐ *Watch several newscasts, listening for carefully worded, diplomatic comments made about or made between heads of state.*

☐ *Use a student's tactless comment or question as a springboard for a good-natured discussion with the class about the importance of tactfulness.*

☐ *Carefully craft a tactfully worded memo or e-mail addressing a concern you've been hesitant to bring up to the administration.*

Things to Remember

A wicked messenger falls into trouble, but a faithful ambassador brings health.

PROVERBS 13:17 NKJV

For love's sake I prefer to appeal to you just for what I am—I, Paul, an ambassador [of Christ Jesus] and an old man and now a prisoner for His sake also.

PHILEMON 1:9 AMP

I have heard a message from the LORD, and an ambassador has been sent to the nations: "Gather together, come against her, and rise up to battle!"

JEREMIAH 49:14 NKJV

Paul wrote: "I am an ambassador in chains; that in it I may speak boldly, as I ought to speak."

EPHESIANS 6:20 NKJV

When Arioch, the commander of the king's guard, had gone out to put to death the wise men of Babylon, Daniel spoke to him with wisdom and tact.

DANIEL 2:14 NIV

He called to Him the Twelve [apostles] and began to send them out [as His ambassadors] two by two and gave them authority and power over the unclean spirits.

MARK 6:7 AMP

The secret of man's success resides in his insight into the moods of people, and his tact in dealing with them.
—JOSIAH GILBERT HOLLAND

Tact is the ability to describe others as they see themselves.
—ABRAHAM LINCOLN

Teachability

Lifelong Learning

Do your best to add these things to your lives: to your faith,
add goodness; to your goodness, add knowledge.

—2 PETER 1:5 NCV

Veteran teacher Thomas Carter balked when he read the e-mail: This semester's in-service training day had been scheduled, and leading the sessions would be an expert from an education think tank in Washington, D.C. Mr. Carter read the expert's bio at the bottom of the message and discovered he had earned his master's degree just two years earlier. What could that kid teach a veteran like him? Mr. Carter finished out the day in a somewhat foul mood, annoyed that he was expected to waste an entire day listening to someone who had probably never actually worked in a classroom.

Some of the other teachers shared his lack of enthusiasm, but the more they listened to the presenter and asked him questions, the more they gravitated toward his way of thinking, which involved a creative teaching style that integrated auditory, visual, and kinesthetic learning methods. By the end of the training day, many of the teachers left the building talking enthusiastically about their plans to try out what they had learned. But not Mr.

Carter. He left the way he arrived, and all he could do was watch from the sidelines as one teacher after another reported tremendous progress with some of their most difficult students after implementing the practical ideas they learned during the in-service day.

Mr. Carter had entered the building that day with a closed mind—not a fitting attribute for a teacher—and a bad attitude, and that's pretty much all he left with. Other teachers left the session overflowing with ideas and enthusiasm. But Mr. Carter's pride had stood between him and the opportunity to learn something that could have revitalized his classroom and benefited his students in untold ways.

As a teacher, you try to instill in your students a love of learning. And it may seem unnecessary to remind you that you need to love learning as well. But the reality is that many people, teachers included, have a fairly set idea of what they are willing to learn, when they are willing to learn, and from whom they are willing to learn. That's nearly always attributable to the sin of pride, which is a serious hindrance to a teachable spirit.

Having a teachable spirit requires humility, the ability to acknowledge that there is a great deal you can learn from other people—and from God. Examine your spirit to see how teachable you really are. Be open to learning new things, even if your teacher turns out to be younger than your own children. Just remember—your own students may end up being the best teachers you've ever had.

I Will

Recognize learning for the lifelong activity that it is.

yes _____ _no_ _____

Be as committed to learning as I want my students to be.

yes _____ _no_ _____

Always be open to what God's Spirit has to teach me.

yes _____ _no_ _____

Acknowledge the reality that I learn a great deal from my students.

yes _____ _no_ _____

Never let pride get in the way of learning from others.

yes _____ _no_ _____

Keep my mind sharp by learning new things.

yes _____ _no_ _____

Things to Do

☐ _Ask your colleagues about continuing education seminars they've attended that have improved their teaching skills._

☐ _Consider working toward an advanced degree or taking an education course you weren't able to take in college._

☐ _For the next week, make note of everything you learn from your students and colleagues._

☐ _Subscribe to a teaching journal, either in print or online (ask other teachers for recommendations for your grade level or subject area)._

☐ _Buy or borrow books on tape to listen to during your commute to and from school._

☐ _Make a commitment to memorize entire psalms or other multiverse passages of Scripture, to keep your mind sharp and your spirit nurtured._

Things to Remember

Wise men and women are always learning, always listening for fresh insights.

PROVERBS 18:15 THE MESSAGE

Give instruction to the wise, and they will become wiser still; teach the righteous and they will gain in learning.

PROVERBS 9:9 NRSV

If you stop learning, you will forget what you already know.

PROVERBS 19:27 CEV

This is what the prophets meant when they wrote, "And then they will all be personally taught by God." Anyone who has spent any time at all listening to the Father, really listening and therefore learning, comes to me to be taught personally—to see it with his own eyes, hear it with his own ears, from me, since I have it firsthand from the Father.

JOHN 6:45 THE MESSAGE

I pray that God will be kind to you and will let you live in perfect peace! May you keep learning more and more about God and our Lord Jesus.

2 PETER 1:2 CEV

There is no time of life past learning something.

—SAINT AMBROSE

He who dares to teach must never cease to learn.

—JOHN COTTON DANA

Finding Strength

Better Than Barbells

The psalmist wrote: "In the day when I cried out, You answered me, and made me bold with strength in my soul."

—Psalm 138:3 NKJV

Beth Stephens could hardly stand the thought of getting out of bed, not to mention the thirty-minute commute and thirty first-graders that awaited her. *Three more weeks*, she thought, *but I don't know if I'll make it this year.*

The end of the school year was always a difficult time for teachers and students alike—so much to do and everyone itching for summer vacation to start. But this year had been especially brutal. The winter had been the worst and the longest in memory, with snow right through the end of April. For a first-grade teacher, that meant lots of pulling and pushing and tugging at multiple layers of footwear and outerwear— helping children still too young to help themselves. Cabin fever seemed to be at an all-time high.

What made things even more trying for Beth was coming home at night to an equally strained and exhausted husband. Jim taught chemistry, and the juniors and seniors in his class were giving him fits—when they were there. A lake nearby seemed to be calling their names—oddly, though, only on warm and sunny days—and those days turned into a guessing game to determine if anyone would actually show up for class. Beth almost wished her students would do the same, as rambunctious as they were. Corralling them to go inside and then settle down at the start of the day, after lunch, and after recess had proven to be an overwhelming task.

Everyone was on edge, and the tension was taking its toll on the Stephenses' marriage. One Friday afternoon, Jim took the long way home, stopping at one of his favorite lakeside spots. He just wanted to be alone and decompress before going home, but the serenity of the site—and the gentle nudging of God's Spirit—gave him more than he expected. As his mind wandered, he slowly came to the realization that unless he and Beth made a radical change, things would only get worse. He prayed and then prayed some more.

Back at home, a cranky Beth started asking where he had been, what he'd been doing, why he wasn't home on time—questions that were so out of character for her. Without a word, Jim began massaging her shoulders and did not stop until he felt the tension begin to melt away. Then he explained his absence. "Let's go for a walk," he suggested. As they walked, he shared with Beth all the insights he felt God had given him as he sat thinking and praying at the lake. They had been trying to get through one of the roughest times in their marriage in their own strength, he said. They were both physically, mentally, and emotionally exhausted. They needed to draw on God's strength and stop using up what little reserves of energy they had left, and they had to recharge their spiritual batteries if they were going to make it through the end of the school year, and through the rest of their lives, with their marriage intact.

Few teachers are spared the occasional feeling that they're close to running out of steam. The end of the year is a particularly vulnerable time for that, but the feeling that you don't have the strength to go on can hit you at any time, often without warning. Taking preventive measures is the best course of action, but if you find yourself close to running on empty, stop immediately and deal with the situation. How? First, by doing what Jim did—decompress in the presence of God. Allow His refreshing Spirit to wash over you and fill you up again, not only with spiritual and emotional strength but also with clear direction in practical ways. For the Stephenses, that meant taking walks together every night, for both exercise and relaxation, and slowing down at home, canceling any unnecessary activities and spending quiet evenings with each other, reading Scripture, praying, and just *being*.

God has promised to give you the strength you need, and He always makes good on His promises. Draw on His strength to build up your own. You'll have what it takes to make it to the end, with energy to spare.

I Will

Rely on God to be the strength of my life.

yes _____ _no_ _____

Acknowledge that my natural strengths are gifts from God.

yes _____ _no_ _____

Strengthen my relationship with God by spending more time with Him.

yes _____ _no_ _____

Accept the fact that I have weaknesses.

yes _____ _no_ _____

Recognize my weaknesses as opportunities for God to give me His strength.

yes _____ _no_ _____

Learn to draw on loved ones for strength when I need to.

yes _____ _no_ _____

Things to Do

☐ _Identify your strengths and weaknesses as a teacher, and research ways you can overcome your weaknesses._

☐ _Honestly define the things you turn to when your emotional strength begins to sag, and resolve to begin turning to God first._

☐ _Use an online concordance to find scriptural references to God giving strength to His people._

☐ _List at least three things you can do to become stronger spiritually— and do them._

☐ _Begin a strength-training program that's appropriate for your age and fitness level._

☐ _Memorize Philippians 4:13._

☐ _Reflect on all of the people you are able to draw strength from, and let them know how important they are to you._

Things to Remember

Jesus said: "You shall love the LORD your God with all your heart, with all your soul, with all your mind, and with all your strength. This is the first commandment."

MARK 12:30 NKJV

Nehemiah told the people, "Enjoy your good food and wine and share some with those who didn't have anything to bring. Don't be sad! This is a special day for the LORD, and he will make you happy and strong."

NEHEMIAH 8:10 CEV

*I can do all things through Christ
who strengthens me.*
Philippians 4:13 NKJV

They go from strength to strength, each one appears before God in Zion.

PSALM 84:7 NKJV

She girds herself with strength, and strengthens her arms.

PROVERBS 31:17 NKJV

The LORD said, "Do not fear, for I am with you; do not be dismayed, for I am your God. I will strengthen you and help you; I will uphold you with my righteous right hand."

ISAIAH 41:10 NIV

Be strong in the Lord and in the power of His might.

EPHESIANS 6:10 NKJV

As your days, so shall your strength be.

DEUTERONOMY 33:25 NKJV

If you falter in times of trouble, how small is your strength!

PROVERBS 24:10 NIV

David wrote: "He is the God who makes me strong, who makes my pathway safe."

PSALM 18:32 GNT

The psalmist wrote: "God is our refuge and strength, an ever-present help in trouble."

PSALM 46:1 NIV

Asaph wrote: "My flesh and my heart may fail, but God is the strength of my heart and my portion forever."

PSALM 73:26 NIV

Trials, temptations, disappointments . . . not only test the fiber of character but strengthen it. Every conquering temptation represents a new fund of moral energy. Every trial endured and weathered in the right spirit makes a soul nobler and stronger than it was before.

—JAMES BUCKHAM

In all my perplexities and distresses, the Bible has never failed to give me light and strength.

—ROBERT E. LEE

Envy

Desire Gone Wrong

Let us not become conceited, provoking one another, envying one another.

—GALATIANS 5:26 NKJV

For the second year in a row, Mr. Harrison had been selected Teacher of the Year at his school—and for the second year in a row, he had deserved the accolade and the grant money that accompanied it. Few people could argue with his success. As an English teacher in an inner-city high school, he had exposed at-risk students to the writings of the great minds throughout history, giving them a vision for their future that promised to turn their lives around. He had even taught them enough Latin to noticeably improve their SAT scores on the verbal portion of the test. As a teacher, he was truly an inspiration to his students.

As for the award, some of the teachers recognized it for the honor it was, while others dismissed it as a popularity contest. Still others—Mrs. Gordon in particular—had a difficult time with it. She had held that honor for two consecutive years before Mr. Harrison arrived, and she had been struggling with envy once again. She had recovered readily enough the previous year, but this year she was counting on the grant to fund the research she had wanted to do at a university library halfway across the country. The envy she had never adequately dealt with last year was greatly multiplied this year.

But this year was different in one significant respect: Mrs. Gordon decided to talk to a counselor at her church, a woman who had helped her deal with a family crisis earlier in the year. The counselor carefully led her through the Scriptures that dealt with envy, showing her just how serious a sin God considered envy to be, but always emphasizing God's mercy and ability to soften and transform a hard and bitter heart. Through prayer, Bible reading, and several counseling sessions, Mrs. Gordon was able to release her feelings of envy once and for all, and begin the slow process of learning to be content with all God had given her—including the money she needed for her summer research, which He provided in a completely unexpected way.

Envy is one of those sins that just doesn't look good on anyone. It always seems to make itself known no matter how much you try to hide it, and when it does, it shows just how unattractive it is. Even worse, it robs you of your peace, your joy, and your intimacy with God, and damages your relationships with other people. Learning contentment may take a lifetime, but that's another gift from God—a lifetime to learn contentment.

I Will

	yes	no
Be content with what I have.	___	___
Immediately turn over to God any envious feelings I have.	___	___
Ask God to restore relationships that may have been damaged by my envious attitude.	___	___
Believe that God has given me everything I need right now.	___	___
Fill my life to overflowing with the things that matter, the things of God.	___	___
Cultivate a thankful spirit.	___	___
Recognize the disunity and strife that envy causes in the family of God.	___	___

Things to Do

☐ List every source of envy in your life, including both material possessions and spiritual gifts that others have and you desire, asking God to change your heart.

☐ List everything you can think of that God has given you—everything. This list should be a lot longer than the preceding one. Thank God for all His gifts.

☐ As evidence of the problem of envy in the early church, use a concordance to count the number of times the word envy appears in the Epistles.

☐ Rid your house of things that provoke envy—such as magazines devoted to luxury homes or bodybuilding or fast cars or skinny models, depending on your particular envy challenge.

Things to Remember

So clean house! Make a clean sweep of malice and pretense, envy and hurtful talk.

1 PETER 2:1 THE MESSAGE

Let us walk properly, as in the day, not in revelry and drunkenness, not in lewdness and lust, not in strife and envy.

ROMANS 13:13 NKJV

Don't for a minute envy careless rebels; soak yourself in the Fear-of-God.

PROVERBS 23:17 THE MESSAGE

A sound heart is life to the body, but envy is rottenness to the bones.

PROVERBS 14:30 NKJV

Then I observed all the work and ambition motivated by envy. What a waste! Smoke. And spitting into the wind.

ECCLESIASTES 4:4 THE MESSAGE

Stop your anger! Turn from your rage! Do not envy others—it only leads to harm.

PSALM 37:8 NLT

Nothing sharpens sight like envy.
—THOMAS FULLER

The sure mark of one born with noble qualities is being born without envy.
—FRANCOIS DE LA ROCHEFOUCAULD

Ethics

Walking Uprightly

LORD, who may abide in Your tabernacle? Who may dwell in Your holy hill? He who walks uprightly, and works righteousness, and speaks the truth in his heart.

—PSALM 15:1–2 NKJV

It's been said that the code of ethics you really live by is evidenced by what you do when no one's looking. In other words, people may say they live according to a high ethical standard, but what they do when no one else is around is a more accurate indicator of their true code of ethics.

You see evidence of this in your own profession: A teacher views pornographic images on a school computer, not realizing that investigators would be able to access information on the sites he visited that was stored on the hard drive. A married teacher and mother of two children has a clandestine affair with a thirteen-year-old student and gives birth to his child in prison. Another teacher is fired after it is discovered that he routinely gave several of the school's star athletes high grades for work that was never done.

Those are all examples of highly unethical behavior, but questionable ethics come into play in far less extreme circumstances as well. In fact, on a daily basis, most people are faced with multiple situations in which they are required to make decisions that reveal the code of ethics they live by. A cashier gives you too much change; a colleague passes along a juicy bit of gossip; a little voice tries to convince you that this is the very last time you'll ever take home any office supplies— honest. How you choose to respond in each of those scenarios is determined by your ethical standard.

As a Christian, you know that your ethics must be above reproach, and you know that there's never a time when no one's looking. In those two respects you already know the importance of doing not only what is right but also what is honorable and pure and just and moral. But knowing it is only half the battle, and the easy half at that.

Living out your high ethical standards requires a moment-by-moment dependence on God's Spirit, the source of the power you need to overcome temptation to do wrong and the wisdom you need to make right choices when the choices aren't all that clear. It requires listening to your God-given conscience and believing that your desire to please God will keep you on the right track. And it requires walking with God—closely and uprightly and continually.

I Will

Remember that the Bible is my best source for ethical guidelines.

yes _____   _no_ _____

Rely on God to lead me to do the right thing.

yes _____   _no_ _____

Place a high priority on ethical behavior.

yes _____   _no_ _____

Realize that others may be looking to me for moral leadership.

yes _____   _no_ _____

Pray for the strength to maintain biblical standards in every area of my life.

yes _____   _no_ _____

Learn from the moral example of Jesus.

yes _____   _no_ _____

Model a godly ethical standard for my students and colleagues.

yes _____   _no_ _____

Things to Do

☐ _Discuss ethics with your students in an appropriate way for their grade level._

☐ _Evaluate the leadership of your teachers' organization and determine how you could contribute toward maintaining a high ethical standard for the group._

☐ _Submit an article on ethical behavior in the classroom to a professional journal or your school district's newsletter._

☐ _Identify three ethical issues in your classroom such as cheating or plagiarizing, research ways of resolving the problems, and implement them as soon as you can._

☐ _Review your school district's code of ethics for faculty, especially noting any omissions that should be added._

Things to Remember

I am guiding you in the way of wisdom, and I am leading you on the right path.

PROVERBS 4:11 NCV

Good people have kind thoughts, but you should never trust the advice of someone evil.

PROVERBS 12:5 CEV

Keep your eyes focused on what is right, and look straight ahead to what is good.

PROVERBS 4:25 NCV

People with good sense know what I say is true; and those with knowledge know my words are right.

PROVERBS 8:9 NCV

Now, everything has been heard, so I give my final advice: Honor God and obey his commands, because this is all people must do. God will judge everything, even what is done in secret, the good and the evil.

ECCLESIASTES 12:13–14 NCV

Be careful what you do, and always do what is right.

PROVERBS 4:26 NCV

Ethics and equity and the principles of justice do not change with the calendar.

—D. H. LAWRENCE

A man without ethics is a wild beast loosed upon this world.

—MANLY HALL

Cooperation

Team Teaching

Two are better than one, because they have a good reward for their labor.

—Ecclesiastes 4:9 NKJV

When Loretta Borden learned that she was going to be asked to participate in an experimental, interdisciplinary team-teaching program, she was more than a little apprehensive. Her students had always responded well when she taught American literature during English class, and now she would be expected to combine her talents with those of an American history teacher. While Jillian Gray was a skilled enough teacher, Mrs. Borden wasn't so sure her class would respond as enthusiastically if Mrs. Gray was present.

Then there was the strategizing they needed to do beforehand: Exactly how would they handle this? Would one teacher do the bulk of instruction on one day, switching off the next? Or would they have equal time during each given class period? They each had a certain amount of material they had to get through over the next few weeks, and this change in the program seemed like an intrusion on their individual instruction time.

As they looked over the guidelines they were to follow, both teachers began bouncing ideas off each other, somewhat tentatively at first. To Mrs. Borden's surprise, the history teacher was thoroughly familiar with the writers of the Civil War era, the period the class would be studying during their team-teaching experiment, and helped the English teacher understand some of the more subtle political issues that played a role in the events before, during, and after the war—issues that helped her gain a different perspective on some of the essayists of that time. Soon enough, their discussion became animated and lively, and in no time, they had developed what they hoped would be the ideal strategy.

The true test, though, would come the following week, when they would start teaching together for real. Their strategy worked beautifully. The students were so intrigued by the teachers' friendly banter that they ended up learning a great deal without realizing it. But it wasn't only the students who learned from the experiment; both teachers, whose teaching styles had been distinctly different, learned a great deal about the need for give and take on a professional level. In fact, both teachers cited "cooperation" as the most important element contributing to the success of the program.

Cooperating with your peers on a professional level is not necessarily an easy thing to do. You are accustomed to being the one in control in your classroom, and presumably you feel you know your field well, and you know the best methods for teaching that subject or grade level. When you're asked to let go of some of that control and share it with another teacher, a lot of factors can come into play that may make you feel apprehensive. Some, like ego and pride, are negative factors, but there are also positive factors like genuine concern for the students and what is best for them. It doesn't have to be a team-teaching situation that causes you to feel uneasy; any circumstance in which you are expected to cooperate on a project with another person is potentially upsetting.

For Christians, another factor comes into play: the concern that they will be asked to compromise their values if they are teamed up with someone who does not believe as they do. Usually, that fear is ungrounded; true compromise involves deeply held convictions rather than preferences or opinions. Most of the time you can cooperate with others without fear of compromise, and you'll likely be aware of the threat of compromise long before you're asked to cross a line you know you can never cross.

Until you reach that line, though, you can provide an example to others of the tremendous amount of good that can be accomplished when people lay aside their fears and their pride and decide to cooperate with each other. When the spirit of cooperation—and an overriding desire for unity—is activated in God's people, there seems to be no limit to what they can accomplish, whether it's in a classroom of twenty children or on a mission field of millions of people.

I Will

Develop and maintain a cooperative spirit.   *yes*   *no*

Encourage cooperation among my peers.   *yes*   *no*

Use teaching opportunities to foster cooperation
in the classroom.   *yes*   *no*

Cooperate with the work of God's Spirit in my life.   *yes*   *no*

Recognize the value of being a team player.   *yes*   *no*

Understand the distinction between healthy
cooperation and unhealthy compromise.   *yes*   *no*

Things to Do

☐ *Create a lesson for your students that will require them to cooperate in order to succeed in accomplishing a particular goal.*

☐ *List some practical steps you personally can take to promote a cooperative spirit among the members of the faculty at your school.*

☐ *Discover how unity among believers affected the world around them, in Acts 2:40–47.*

☐ *Develop a team-teaching proposal and discuss it with your peers before presenting it to the administration.*

☐ *Get together with several other teachers to talk about the successful methods you've used to get your students to cooperate with you and with each other.*

☐ *Reflect on a situation in which your fear of compromise unwittingly made you uncooperative—or your desire to cooperate resulted in compromise.*

Things to Remember

Don't be hateful and insult people just because they are hateful and insult you. Instead, treat everyone with kindness. You are God's chosen ones, and he will bless you.

1 PETER 3:9 CEV

Speaking the truth in love, [you] may grow up in all things into Him who is the head—Christ.

EPHESIANS 4:15 NKJV

Behold, how good and how pleasant it is for brethren to dwell together in unity!
Psalm 133:1 NKJV

Now the multitude of those who believed were of one heart and one soul; neither did anyone say that any of the things he possessed was his own, but they had all things in common.

ACTS 4:32 NKJV

He who serves Christ in these things is acceptable to God and approved by men. Therefore let us pursue the things which make for peace and the things by which one may edify another.

ROMANS 14:18–19 NKJV

There is one body and one Spirit, just as you were called in one hope of your calling.

EPHESIANS 4:4 NKJV

Paul wrote: "Let your conduct be worthy of the gospel of Christ, so that whether I come and see you or am absent, I may hear of your affairs, that you stand fast in one spirit, with one mind striving together for the faith of the gospel."

PHILIPPIANS 1:27 NKJV

Paul wrote: "I urge you to pay all deference to such leaders and to enlist under them and be subject to them, as well as to everyone who joins and cooperates [with you] and labors earnestly."

1 CORINTHIANS 16:16 AMP

Paul wrote: "You also cooperate by your prayers for us [helping and laboring together with us]. Thus [the lips of] many persons [turned toward God will eventually] give thanks on our behalf for the grace (the blessing of deliverance) granted us at the request of the many who have prayed."

2 CORINTHIANS 1:11 AMP

We ourselves ought to support such people [to welcome and provide for them], in order that we may be fellow workers in the Truth (the whole Gospel) and cooperate with its teachers.

3 JOHN 1:8 AMP

It is one of the beautiful compensations of this life that no one can sincerely try to help another without helping himself.

—CHARLES DUDLEY

It is through cooperation, rather than conflict, that your greatest successes will be derived.

—RALPH CHARELL

Planning

Looking Ahead

My child, don't lose sight of good planning and insight. Hang on to them.

—PROVERBS 3:21 NLT

Imagine announcing a daylong field trip to the Smithsonian in Washington, D.C., to an entire class of fifth-graders from a suburban school in nearby Virginia—but failing to make plans for the day. There would be no buses, no itinerary, no chaperones, no money, no list of must-see exhibits. In short, there would be no trip, just several hundred disappointed children waiting in the parking lot, wondering why they got excited for nothing.

You wouldn't do that, of course. But while it's unlikely that any school can cite such an extreme example of lack of planning, most teachers can recall situations in which someone dropped the ball and failed to make plans or follow through on plans that were made, and the results were disappointing at best.

You may understand completely how important planning is to your job as a teacher. But you may not understand as fully just how important planning is to your life. Many people are so busy and so preoccupied that they simply go through the motions of living. Maybe you're one of them. If so, spending some time planning your life can enable you to actually live instead of going through the motions.

Start by asking God what His plans are for you. Then give some thought to what you would like to be doing in five or ten or twenty years, see how your desires line up with what God has shown you, and make adjustments accordingly.

For example, maybe God has given you a vision for reaching university students for Christ. You'll need an advanced degree and college-level teaching experience that wasn't on your radar screen. But your God-given vision is so strong that you need to do some serious planning toward attaining the goal He has placed before you.

Now you need to break that large goal down into smaller steps by developing a series of shorter-term plans. You can devote the next three to six months, for instance, to researching online master's programs that will allow you to continue working. The next step might be to talk with graduates of those programs, and then apply to one you select. Instead of focusing exclusively on the larger goal, you'll find a great deal more satisfaction in narrowing your focus to achievable steps along the way.

Just make sure you keep consulting God about your plans. Things have a way of changing, and He's the One you need to be talking to if you experience a midcourse correction. Keep your plans in mind, but keep your eyes on God.

I Will

Make plans according to God's leading.   yes _____   no _____

Take others into consideration when planning.   yes _____   no _____

Be open to God-inspired changes in my plans.   yes _____   no _____

Make both short-term and long-range plans.   yes _____   no _____

Expect my God-ordained plans to succeed.   yes _____   no _____

Divide larger plans into smaller steps.   yes _____   no _____

Recognize the timesaving benefits of planning.   yes _____   no _____

Things to Do

☐ Memorize all of Psalm 1.

☐ As you're doing your lesson plans for the coming week, create a plan for your personal activities as well.

☐ Meditate on Jeremiah 29:11 and what that means for your life.

☐ Begin planning a project that you have been putting off.

☐ Enlist your students' help in planning a project that will teach them as much about planning as it does the subject matter.

☐ Find appropriate quotations about planning in a quotation book and post them around your classroom.

☐ Reflect on the pleasure God took in planning your adoption into His family (see Ephesians 1:5).

Things to Remember

Jesus said, "I'm no longer calling you servants because servants don't understand what their master is thinking and planning. No, I've named you friends because I've let you in on everything I've heard from the Father."

JOHN 15:15 THE MESSAGE

Who ever knows what you're thinking and planning except you yourself? The same with God—except that he not only knows what he's thinking, but he lets us in on it. God offers a full report on the gifts of life and salvation that he is giving us.

1 CORINTHIANS 2:11–12 THE MESSAGE

Long, long ago he decided to adopt us into his family through Jesus Christ. (What pleasure he took in planning this!)

EPHESIANS 1:5 THE MESSAGE

Jesus said, "When he brings out his own sheep, he goes before them; and the sheep follow him, for they know his voice."

JOHN 10:4 NKJV

In this way they will store up for themselves a treasure which will be a solid foundation for the future. And then they will be able to win the life which is true life.

1 TIMOTHY 6:19 GNT

If you don't design your own life plan, chances are you'll fall into someone else's plan. And guess what they have planned for you? Not much.
—JIM ROHN

Plan your work for today and every day, then work your plan.
—NORMAN VINCENT PEALE

Servanthood

Class Rank

Jesus said, "For even the Son of Man did not come to be served, but to serve, and to give His life a ransom for many."
—MARK 10:45 NKJV

A great deal has been written and preached about servanthood in recent years, thanks in large part to the spread of a concept known as servant leadership—the understanding that the best leaders are those who serve their followers rather than expect their followers to serve them. As a teacher, you are already a leader, and there's a significant likelihood that you also have a servant's spirit. Few people would enter the teaching profession without that quality, at least in the beginning of their career.

Through the years, though, a teacher's servant spirit can become jaded by the overwhelming responsibilities of the job or even corrupted by promotions, accolades, and honors. It may be time to put the servant spirit back into the leader, something that is fortunately not a difficult task at all for the One who gives teachers their servant spirit to begin with.

As you cooperate with God, He will restore the quality of servanthood to your life. Begin by asking Him to renew the passion you once had for serving others, primarily the students you see every day. Look at the way Jesus, the master Teacher, related to His students, the disciples. Learn from Him and apply what you learn to the way you relate to your students, given their ages and maturity level. Ask God for creative ways to be of service both in the classroom and throughout the campus, to the student body at large, the faculty, and the rest of the staff.

All those qualities that go into making a servant leader—humility, empathy, compassion, and many more—will come with time, as you become responsive to God's leading and find yourself automatically doing unusual-for-you things, like pouring coffee for the other teachers in the lounge or calling a single parent at home and offering to tutor her child to help lighten her load. You'll probably experience joy on a whole new level as you discover more and more ways to serve others.

If you would like to find out more about servant leadership, you can enter the term into a search engine and find numerous Web sites devoted to the biblical qualities of a servant leader. Or you can simply open your Bible and read about Moses, Joshua, and other servant leaders, the first and foremost being Jesus Himself. From their examples, you'll discover the characteristics of a model servant leader, the only kind of leader whose example is worth following.

I Will

Cultivate a servant spirit.   _yes_   _no_

Realize that I am on earth to serve rather than
to be served.   _yes_   _no_

Find creative ways to serve others.   _yes_   _no_

Recognize the opportunities I already have to
serve others.   _yes_   _no_

Be willing to serve where needed at church.   _yes_   _no_

Follow Jesus' example of a servant leader.   _yes_   _no_

Draw others to God by serving them.   _yes_   _no_

Things to Do

 List three things you can do during the school day to model servanthood for your students.

 Learn about servant leadership through a Web site such as www.servleader.org.

☐ *Try out a new way to serve at your church.*

☐ *Read about the qualities of a servant in Ephesians 6:1–9.*

☐ *Reflect on what it meant for Jesus to come to earth in human form so He could serve you.*

☐ *Organize a schoolwide service project or become involved in an ongoing project.*

 Perform an act of service for someone who normally serves you, such as a teacher aide.

Things to Remember

Jesus said, "The master answered, 'You did well. You are a good and loyal servant. Because you were loyal with small things, I will let you care for much greater things. Come and share my joy with me.' "

MATTHEW 25:23 NCV

O may Your lovingkindness comfort me, according to Your word to Your servant.

PSALM 119:76 NASB

The LORD came and stood there, calling as at the other times, "Samuel! Samuel!" Then Samuel said, "Speak, for your servant is listening."

1 SAMUEL 3:10 NIV

> If we do not lay out ourselves in the service of mankind, whom should we serve?
> —JOHN ADAMS

[Jesus], being in very nature God, did not consider equality with God something to be grasped, but made himself nothing, taking the very nature of a servant, being made in human likeness.

PHILIPPIANS 2:6–7 NIV

> To serve is beautiful, but only if it is done with joy and a whole heart and a free mind.
> —PEARL S. BUCK

Jesus said to them, "The kings of the Gentiles lord it over them; and those who have authority over them are called 'Benefactors.' But it is not this way with you, but the one who is the greatest among you must become like the youngest, and the leader like the servant."

LUKE 22:25–26 NASB

Grace

Unmerited Favor

God is able to make all grace abound toward you, that you, always having all sufficiency in all things, may have an abundance for every good work.

—2 CORINTHIANS 9:8 NKJV

All the students at Woodrow Wilson High School knew about Mr. Fiorentino—how he was a stickler about turning homework in on time and being in the classroom when the bell rang and never, ever interrupting him. His math classes were no harder than the other classes were, but *he* was harder; the man was tough as nails, and each semester the guidance counselors prepared themselves for the steady stream of students trying to get their schedules changed to avoid having him as their teacher.

Michael Fiorentino was well aware of what the students, and the overworked guidance counselors, thought about his approach to teaching. What they did not know was that Mr. Fiorentino had spent time over the Christmas break with one of his former high school math teachers, and as they talked, the younger teacher finally began to realize that he was undermining his effectiveness as a teacher by being so strict. When school resumed in January, though, there seemed to be no change in his methods.

"You'll have your written reports on the high cost of consumer debt on my desk no later than January 22," he told his consumer math classes. "And that means by the time the bell rings at the beginning of your class period on January 22." He sounded as strict as ever.

Sure enough, when January 22 rolled around, Mr. Fiorentino stood guard over his desk at the beginning of each class period. "On time" papers went into one pile; "after bell" papers went into another. A note from the office explaining one student's tardiness went straight in the trash. The latecomers figured they were doomed.

Three weeks went by, and still he hadn't returned the graded reports. The marking period was drawing to a close; the written reports represented a significant percentage of the students' grades, but no one had received an interim grade. Finally, one month to the day later, Mr. Fiorentino made an announcement at the start of each class period. He was returning the reports, he said, and each student had been graded on the quality of the report. No points were deducted for late submissions. As the students sat stunned, their teacher used the reports as an object lesson on grace—specifically, the thirty-day grace period credit card companies extend to their cardholders. It was a lesson in consumer math that the students never forgot, especially those students who expected to be penalized but discovered their papers were not considered late after all. That day marked the end of their teacher's "tough as nails" approach to teaching.

Maybe you've never been known as a strict teacher. Maybe you're even considered by some of the other teachers to be a bit too soft on the kids. Regardless of your reputation or teaching style, you can take advantage of numerous opportunities to extend grace—an undeserved reward, gift, or privilege—to your students. God's gift of salvation is a prime example of grace, a gift that no person ever deserved but one that He offers to all people. Any time you give your students an undeserved reward or privilege, you are giving them a real-life example, on the level of their understanding, of the kind of grace God gives.

Consider this: If every student in the school suddenly decided to play hooky, and the school decided not to punish them but allow them to return to class without any negative ramifications, that would be an example of grace. Students—as well as adults—need to understand that there are consequences for their behavior, and extending grace on a regular basis won't help prepare them for the real world. The Israelites suffered the consequences of their rebellion against God, but their leaders—the godly ones, anyway—held out hope for God's grace, confident He would bestow undeserved favor on them. You've suffered the consequences for your own rebellion, but you've also experienced the immeasurable grace God bestowed on you when you came to faith in Christ. There's a lesson in grace awaiting your students, even if you never mention the name of Jesus.

I Will

	yes	no
Receive God's gift of grace.	_yes_	_no_
Be thankful to God for extending grace to me.	_yes_	_no_
Return the favor by extending grace to others.	_yes_	_no_
Believe that I have done nothing, and can do nothing, to earn God's grace.	_yes_	_no_
Show my gratitude by living a Christ-honoring life.	_yes_	_no_
Tell others about God's grace.	_yes_	_no_
Never take His grace for granted.	_yes_	_no_

Things to Do

☐ *Demonstrate the concept of grace for your students in a practical way, such as erasing the lowest test score each student received during one marking period.*

☐ *Use the parable of the prodigal son in Luke 15 to describe grace to someone unfamiliar with the concept.*

☐ *Reflect on the last time God gave you something that you didn't deserve, and spend time in prayer thanking Him for it.*

☐ *Read Paul's explanation of the grace of God, and what it means for a believer, in Romans 6.*

☐ *Compare the dictionary definition with a biblical understanding of grace.*

☐ *Help several friends or colleagues see how God's grace has impacted their lives.*

Things to Remember

From the standpoint of the gospel [the Jews] are enemies for your sake, but from the standpoint of God's choice they are beloved for the sake of the fathers; for the gifts and the calling of God are irrevocable.

ROMANS 11:28–29 NASB

I wrote to encourage you and to tell you that this is the true grace of God. Stand strong in that grace.

1 PETER 5:12 NCV

Sin shall not have dominion over you, for you are not under law but under grace.
Romans 6:14 NKJV

God's grace and order wins; godlessness loses.

PSALM 10:16 THE MESSAGE

What should we do? Should we sin because we are under grace and not under law? No!

ROMANS 6:15 NCV

Paul wrote: "Now this is our boast: Our conscience testifies that we have conducted ourselves in the world, and especially in our relations with you, in the holiness and sincerity that are from God. We have done so not according to worldly wisdom but according to God's grace."

2 CORINTHIANS 1:12 NIV

Sunrise breaks through the darkness for good people—God's grace and mercy and justice!

PSALM 112:4 THE MESSAGE

May the God of all grace, who called us to His eternal glory by Christ Jesus, after you have suffered a while, perfect, establish, strengthen, and settle you.

1 PETER 5:10 NKJV

God is good to one and all; everything he does is suffused with grace.

PSALM 145:9 THE MESSAGE

Paul wrote: "According to the grace of God which was given to me, as a wise master builder I have laid the foundation, and another builds on it. But let each one take heed how he builds on it."

1 CORINTHIANS 3:10 NKJV

God treats us much better than we deserve, and because of Christ Jesus, he freely accepts us and sets us free from our sins.

ROMANS 3:24 CEV

Still, because of your great compassion, you didn't make a total end to them. You didn't walk out and leave them for good; yes, you are a God of grace and compassion.

NEHEMIAH 9:31 THE MESSAGE

Grace is free sovereign favor to the ill-deserving.

—BENJAMIN B. WARFIELD

Grace has been defined as the outward expression of the inward harmony of the soul.

—WILLIAM HAZLITT

Encouragement

Personal Cheerleader

Encourage each other every day while it is "today." Help each other so none of you will become hardened because sin has tricked you.

—Hebrews 3:13 NCV

A simple word of encouragement can make all the difference in a person's day. You've probably seen this for yourself. You'll be plodding along, discouraged by your students' lack of interest or a colleague's pettiness or your spouse's insensitivity. Then someone compliments you on your exceptional handling of a difficult student or a colleague e-mails a no-occasion-but-friendship card or you find a note your husband tucked in your purse just to cheer you up. What happens? Your entire day changes. The smile returns to your face, and you walk a little taller and straighter. You've been encouraged.

Encouragement is a gift you can give to anyone, at any time, in any place—including yourself, right now, right here. If you're feeling discouraged, think back to all the times God has come through for you. Then think ahead to all He has promised you. Finally, look around at all He has given you at this very moment. Still discouraged? Open your Bible to the psalms and start reading. Listen to some praise music. Listen to the voice of God. Go do something unexpected for a neighbor or a colleague. Your discouragement will eventually lift—and if no one has come by to encourage you in the meantime, you'll realize just how important your words of encouragement can be to another person's life.

Everyone needs your encouragement, but perhaps no one needs it as much as your students do. Most teachers are all too aware of the children in their classrooms who seldom hear any words of praise or approval or support. They need all the encouragement they can get. Even the overachievers, who may be experiencing an enormous amount of pressure to perform, could stand to hear someone tell them they're terrific just the way they are. To be effective, your encouragement needs to be sincere, of course; praising a child who crossed the finish line dead last only makes her feel worse. And the more specific your encouragement is, the better. A colleague would much rather hear "Your speech convinced me that we need to reconsider the school board's proposal" than "But of course it was a good speech!"

It can be hard to be an encourager; some people don't know how to accept your words of support, while others may prefer that you commiserate with them. Keep encouraging them, but keep your eyes and ears and heart open for those who welcome the thought of having their own personal cheerleader, a person who is content to stand on the sidelines cheering them on to victory.

I Will

Be an example of encouragement to others. _____ yes _____ no

Learn to encourage myself. _____ yes _____ no

Give my discouragement to God. _____ yes _____ no

Encourage rather than criticize my students. _____ yes _____ no

Be someone else's personal cheerleader. _____ yes _____ no

Build others up without being envious. _____ yes _____ no

Believe God's Spirit will encourage the people I'm praying for. _____ yes _____ no

Things to Do

☐ *Create an appropriate rewards program to recognize achievement and encourage your students.*

☐ *Write an encouraging note or e-mail to someone you know who is going through a rough time.*

☐ *Read the book of Colossians for a glimpse into how Paul encouraged the early church.*

☐ *Think of at least three things you can do to encourage a colleague, and do one of them immediately.*

☐ *Send an encouraging letter to the parents of the students in your class.*

☐ *Become someone's personal cheerleader by beginning the habit of regularly calling to offer words of encouragement.*

☐ *Start a list of Bible verses you can turn to when you feel discouraged.*

Things to Remember

Now may the God Who gives the power of patient endurance (steadfastness) and Who supplies encouragement, grant you to live in such mutual harmony and such full sympathy with one another, in accord with Christ Jesus.

ROMANS 15:5 AMP

Paul wrote: "We constantly pray for you, that our God may count you worthy of his calling, and that by his power he may fulfill every good purpose of yours and every act prompted by your faith."

2 THESSALONIANS 1:11 NIV

Encourage (admonish, exhort) one another and edify (strengthen and build up) one another, just as you are doing.

1 THESSALONIANS 5:11 AMP

Whoever has the gift of encouraging others should encourage.

ROMANS 12:8 NCV

Paul wrote: "We earnestly beseech you, brethren, admonish (warn and seriously advise) those who are out of line [the loafers, the disorderly, and the unruly]; encourage the timid and fainthearted, help and give your support to the weak souls, [and] be very patient with everybody [always keeping your temper]."

1 THESSALONIANS 5:14 AMP

There are high spots in all of our lives and most of them have come about through encouragement from someone else.
—GEORGE M. ADAMS

Flatter me, and I may not believe you. Criticize me, and I may not like you. Ignore me, and I may not forgive you. Encourage me, and I may not forget you.
—WILLIAM ARTHUR

Joy

Beyond Happiness

This is the day the LORD has made; we will rejoice and be glad in it.

—PSALM 118:24 NKJV

If you've ever experienced genuine joy, you know that it's a much deeper experience than happiness is. Your ability to feel happy depends on your circumstances; if the sun is shining and all the traffic lights were green on your way to work and a half-dozen people smiled at you as you walked toward your classroom, you might say you feel happy. But joy—that's another thing altogether. When you experience real joy—the kind that bubbles up inside of you and simply won't let go—nothing can take that experience away from you, not a blizzard, not a series of red traffic lights, not a long line of grousing coworkers. Nothing.

That's because true joy comes from knowing God. Not just knowing about Him, but knowing *Him*—knowing His love, His faithfulness, His abiding presence in your life. When you live in a constant awareness of His presence, you live in a place where joy is yours for the taking, no matter what the circumstances.

Look at some contemporary Christians who have experienced joy in the midst of circumstances that appear horrifying to others: Corrie ten Boom, in a Nazi concentration camp, watching her beloved sister waste away and die; Joni Eareckson Tada, enjoying a fun-filled day until a crack in her spine rendered her paralyzed and confined to a wheelchair for life; Gracia Burnham, helplessly watching as her husband bled to death as a result of "friendly fire." Each one testifies to the overwhelming sense of joy they experience in the presence of God.

The circumstances of your life are likely to be far less dramatic than theirs, but your life can still be a testimony to the kind of joy that only God can give. People need to see joy in the midst of divorce or the death of a loved one or even acrimonious salary negotiations. Most people can relate to those kinds of experiences; to see someone just like them who is filled with joy offers them hope that they can escape their lives of "quiet desperation," as Henry David Thoreau put it. You are in the best position to show them how they can have the same kind of joy and hope that you have.

Without even realizing it, you may already be spreading joy to others. It doesn't matter whether you think your joy is apparent or not; other people can see the evidence of God's activity in your life in ways that you cannot. Just keep living in His presence, close to the only Source of true joy.

I Will

Rejoice in the Lord.

yes _____ no _____

Make sure I am spreading joy to others.

yes _____ no _____

Realize that I can be joyful even when things
are not going well for me.

yes _____ no _____

Maintain my joy by staying close to God.

yes _____ no _____

Be thankful for everything in my life, both the
good and the bad.

yes _____ no _____

Acknowledge that following God's will helps
determine the measure of joy in my life.

yes _____ no _____

Remain joyful by keeping my mind and heart
turned toward God.

yes _____ no _____

Things to Do

☐ Read about the way the prophet Jeremiah acquired his joy in
Jeremiah 15.

☐ Using a concordance, find several joy-saturated psalms and pray them
back to God.

☐ Practice singing joyfully to the Lord.

☐ Recall a time when you experienced joy in the midst of turmoil and
sadness, and use that experience to encourage a friend who is hurting.

☐ Make a list of the things in your life that bring you the most joy, and
thank God specifically for everything and everyone on the list.

☐ Memorize James 1:2–3: "Consider it all joy, my brethren, when you
encounter various trials, knowing that the testing of your faith
produces endurance" (NASB).

Things to Remember

Serve the LORD with gladness; come before His presence with singing.

PSALM 100:2 NKJV

May the God of hope fill you with all joy and peace as you trust in him, so that you may overflow with hope by the power of the Holy Spirit.

ROMANS 15:13 NIV

You will make known to me the path of life; in Your presence is fullness of joy; in Your right hand there are pleasures forever.

PSALM 16:11 NASB

Jesus said, "Therefore you now have sorrow; but I will see you again and your heart will rejoice, and your joy no one will take from you."

JOHN 16:22 NKJV

Oh come, let us sing to the LORD! Let us shout joyfully to the Rock of our salvation. Let us come before His presence with thanksgiving; let us shout joyfully to Him with psalms.

PSALM 95:1–2 NKJV

The LORD said, "The people who live [in Jerusalem] will sing praise; they will shout for joy. By my blessing they will increase in numbers; my blessing will bring them honor."

JEREMIAH 30:19 GNT

The surest mark of a Christian is not faith, or even love, but joy.

—SAMUEL M. SHOEMAKER

Joy is a net of love by which you can catch souls. A joyful heart is the inevitable result of a heart burning with love.

—MOTHER TERESA

Vision

Eyes That See

Where there is no vision, the people perish.

—PROVERBS 29:18 KJV

Every teacher has heard the stories: An inner-city teacher takes a classroom full of at-risk underachievers and has them performing Shakespeare in two months' time. Another teacher in a rural, backwater region turns her barely literate middle-schoolers into statewide science fair winners. Before long, teachers across the country are trying to achieve those kinds of results. But their likelihood of succeeding is limited unless they instill a sense of vision in their students.

Teachers who see dramatic turnarounds in their students are those who understand that like adults, children need a purpose and a hope for their future that is much larger than anything they can see at the moment. They need a vision: a clear picture of what can be, something that is attainable and achievable and desirable. Having them perform Shakespeare isn't enough; inspiring them to accomplish something that others had determined was so far out of their reach provides them with a vision for all those other things they can accomplish in life—things other people told them they could never do.

A case in point is Peter, the product of an abusive home who began living on the streets when he was twelve. School provided him with seven hours of warmth and shelter and two meals a day; beyond that, he had little use for school until one day when Mrs. Halpern confiscated a notebook Peter had thrown at another student. Peter lunged toward her to retrieve the notebook. Another teacher intervened, hauling Peter off to the office. Although Mrs. Halpern was shaken by the incident, she couldn't take her eyes off the notebook that had fallen open on the floor, revealing Peter's disturbing but powerful drawings.

Through time—actually, a great deal of time—Mrs. Halpern convinced Peter that he was not only talented, but exceptionally talented. She gradually helped him catch a vision for what his life could be like, and in the meantime she encouraged him to try to sell his artwork. He did, and with the help of his newfound foster family, he opened a savings account and eventually earned enough to supplement the scholarship money he received for art school. Today he readily acknowledges that if that one teacher had not given him a vision for his future, he would still be on the streets—or in a morgue.

God has likely given you a vision for your own life. If not—if you're not sure what it is—it's time to find out. Meanwhile, make sure you give your students the gift of vision, the ability to see a hope for their future that's as clear as can be.

I Will

Allow God to give me His vision for my future. _____ yes _____ no

Keep that vision in mind during the ordinary
times of my life. _____ yes _____ no

Share the importance of having a vision
with others. _____ yes _____ no

Give my students a general vision for their lives. _____ yes _____ no

Trust God to see to it that my vision comes to pass. _____ yes _____ no

Realize that circumstances may appear to steer me
off course for a while. _____ yes _____ no

Believe that all things work together for good—and
toward seeing my vision fulfilled. _____ yes _____ no

Things to Do

☐ *Ask God to help you see His vision for your life, and write down what
you believe He reveals to you.*

☐ *Share your vision with a trusted friend or colleague and pray together
about each other's vision for the future.*

☐ *Habakkuk 2:2–3 (NLT) says: "Write my answer in large, clear letters
on a tablet, so that a runner can read it and tell everyone else."
Write out your vision clearly and descriptively, so others may
understand what it is.*

☐ *Get together with several teachers and talk about your vision for your
school and your school system.*

☐ *Memorize Philippians 3:7–8: "Christ has shown me that what I once
thought was valuable is worthless. Nothing is as wonderful as knowing
Christ Jesus my Lord. I have given up everything else and count it all
as garbage. All I want is Christ" (CEV).*

Things to Remember

Paul wrote: "I pray that the eyes of your heart may be enlightened, so that you will know what is the hope of His calling, what are the riches of the glory of His inheritance in the saints."

EPHESIANS 1:18 NASB

The noble man makes noble plans, and by noble deeds he stands.

ISAIAH 32:8 NIV

Paul wrote: "We make it our goal to please him, whether we are at home in the body or away from it."

2 CORINTHIANS 5:9 NIV

Therefore . . . I was not disobedient to the heavenly vision.

ACTS 26:19 NKJV

Paul wrote: "Christ has shown me that what I once thought was valuable is worthless. Nothing is as wonderful as knowing Christ Jesus my Lord. I have given up everything else and count it all as garbage. All I want is Christ."

PHILIPPIANS 3:7–8 CEV

Wisdom is in the presence of the one who has understanding, but the eyes of a fool are on the ends of the earth.

PROVERBS 17:24 NASB

He that governs well leads the blind, but he that teaches gives him eyes.

—ROBERT SOUTH

Vision looks inwards and becomes duty. Vision looks outwards and becomes aspiration. Vision looks upwards and becomes faith.

—STEPHEN S. WISE

Celebration

Party Time

They will talk together about the glory of your kingdom; they
will celebrate examples of your power.

—PSALM 145:11 NLT

Party people—they're in every school. They're the
teachers or the administrators who organize the monthly
parties for all those who are celebrating their birthdays
that month. They're the ones who know that Mrs.
Christopher likes white cake with strawberry icing,
Principal Adams prefers German chocolate cake with
walnuts, and Mr. Griffin simply has to have red velvet cake
with cream cheese icing—and they all celebrate their
birthdays in the same month. What on earth will the party
people do now?

There's no need for a celebration to be so complicated. There's not even any need for a celebration to be
tied to a special occasion like a birthday. Is the sun shining
after two whole weeks of cold and rainy weather? That
certainly calls for a celebration. But even better are the
celebrations that acknowledge the little victories that often
go unnoticed in people's lives. A teacher who's been
waiting for the results of some frightening medical tests
deserves a treat when the results come back negative. A

child whose father returns home after fighting in a war overseas could stand a bit of celebrating. And you—don't forget yourself. You need to remember to celebrate, even when no one but you knows about your victories.

The most important element in any celebration is not the food or the decorations, the location or even the occasion itself. The most important element is the people. A simple celebration honoring a coworker who reached tenure, or had an article published in a prestigious education journal, or finally got approval to use the curriculum of her choosing makes the person realize that someone *noticed*, someone paid attention and realized that something important had happened, no matter how minor it may seem to other people.

There's simply no substitute for being attentive to others. When you really pay attention to other people and congratulate them on a little-known accomplishment, they're often stunned to realize that you are aware of what's going on in their lives. Imagine if you called for a celebration! Go ahead and do it, even if the celebration consists of a cup of coffee at a café down the street.

People all around you are starved for genuine, caring attention. By celebrating the big and little milestones in their lives, you show them just how important they are to you—and that often opens the door to showing them just how important they are to God. Go ahead—celebrate! The angels in heaven are rejoicing right along with you.

I Will

Give myself permission to have fun and enjoy life. _____yes_____ _____no_____

Be on the lookout for milestones and occasions for celebration. _____yes_____ _____no_____

Be aware of any tendency I may have to take life too seriously. _____yes_____ _____no_____

Realize that God wants to be a part of my times of celebration. _____yes_____ _____no_____

Rediscover the joy of spontaneous fun. _____yes_____ _____no_____

Thank God for the many sources of pleasure He has provided. _____yes_____ _____no_____

Share my enthusiasm for life with others. _____yes_____ _____no_____

Things to Do

☐ Celebrate the next unusual "national" day—like National Pickle Day—in an appropriately fun way in your classroom.

☐ Come up with a way to celebrate the little things that happen to your students, especially those who seldom receive academic or popular recognition.

☐ Plan an end-of-the-school-year celebration with several other teachers.

☐ Celebrate your relationship with God by spending an entire day alone with Him.

☐ Treat a friend who does not know God to a special event, such as a concert or play or sports competition, just for the fun of it.

☐ List as many things as you can think of that you love to do—even things you haven't done in years—and start doing them again.

Things to Remember

A voice came from the throne, saying, "Praise our God, all you His servants and those who fear Him, both small and great!"

REVELATION 19:5 NKJV

Young women will dance and be glad. And so will the men, young and old alike. I will turn their sobbing into gladness. I will comfort them. And I will give them joy instead of sorrow.

JEREMIAH 31:13 NIrV

Jesus said, "Count on it—that's the kind of party God's angels throw every time one lost soul turns to God."

LUKE 15:10 THE MESSAGE

The ransomed of the LORD shall return, and come to Zion with singing, with everlasting joy on their heads. They shall obtain joy and gladness, and sorrow and sighing shall flee away.

ISAIAH 35:10 NKJV

Neighbors ranging from as far north as Issachar, Zebulun, and Naphtali arrived with donkeys, camels, mules, and oxen loaded down with food for the party: flour, fig cakes, raisin cakes, wine, oil, cattle, and sheep—joy in Israel!

1 CHRONICLES 12:40 THE MESSAGE

Celebrate what you want to see more of.

—THOMAS J. PETERS

We have all eternity to celebrate our victories, but only one short hour before sunset in which to win them.

—ROBERT MOFFAT

Other Books in the *Checklist for Life* Series

Checklist for Life
ISBN 0-7852-6455-8

Checklist for Life for Graduates
ISBN 0-7852-6186-9

Checklist for Life for Leaders
ISBN 0-7852-6001-3

Checklist for Life for Moms
ISBN 0-7852-6004-8

Checklist for Life for Teens
ISBN 0-7852-6461-2

Checklist for Life for Women
ISBN 0-7852-6462-0

Checklist for Life for Men
ISBN 0-7852-6463-9